Jesus Christ~the Alpha & the Omega

Text copyright © Nigel G. Wright 2010
The author asserts the moral right
to be identified as the author of this work

Published by
The Bible Reading Fellowship
15 The Chambers, Vineyard
Abingdon OX14 3FE
United Kingdom
Tel: +44 (0)1865 319700
Email: enquiries@brf.org.uk
Website: www.brf.org.uk
BRF is a Registered Charity

ISBN 978 1 84101 757 0

First published 2010
10 9 8 7 6 5 4 3 2 1 0
All rights reserved

Acknowledgments
Unless otherwise stated, scripture quotations are taken from the New Revised Standard
Version of the Bible, Anglicised Edition, copyright © 1989, 1995 by the Division of Christian
Education of the National Council of the Churches of Christ in the United States of America,
and are used by permission. All rights reserved.

Scripture quotations taken from the Revised Standard Version of the Bible, copyright © 1946,
1952, 1971 by the Division of Christian Education of the National Council of the Churches of
Christ in the United States of America, are used by permission. All rights reserved.

Scripture quotations taken from The Holy Bible, Today's New International Version, copyright
© 2004 by International Bible Society. Used by permission of Hodder & Stoughton Publishers,
a member of the Hachette Livre UK Group. All rights reserved. 'TNIV' is a registered
trademark of International Bible Society.

Page 199: Prayer taken from *The Methodist Worship Book* © 1999 Trustees for Methodist
Church Purposes. Used by permission of Methodist Publishing.

A catalogue record for this book is available from the British Library

Printed in Singapore by Craft Print International Ltd

Nigel G. Wright

Jesus Christ~the Alpha & the Omega

Bible readings and reflections for
Lent and Easter

For Charis,
to say welcome

Contents

Part Two: A journey of discipleship

Introduction

In this book we shall be making two journeys. The first is a journey of discovery in which we shall call to mind the full scope of what Christians believe about Christ. It follows the journey that God in Christ has travelled for the sake of human beings, a journey through which we learn about who the God of Jesus Christ truly is. This first journey will occupy the major part of these daily readings for Lent, 39 of them to be exact, and will touch on many of the foundational Christian convictions about Christ as truly human and fully divine. You will find that the understanding of Christ presented here is in accord with the robust beliefs of mainstream Christian faith, and unashamedly so. Then, in the light of that first journey of discovery, we shall make a second, shorter but no less important one. We may think of this as a journey of discipleship. It will take us to the events of the last week of Jesus' life, beginning on Palm Sunday, events that occupy a disproportionate amount of space in the Gospel narratives, which we recall in Holy Week and which culminated in Christ's death and resurrection. Our purpose here will be to renew our love for Christ and our response in gratitude to him, bearing in mind all that we have understood about him in the course of the journey of discovery. The hope is, therefore, that we shall read these narratives with new depth.

The title chosen for this book seeks to capture the essence of what it is about. Jesus Christ is, according to the New Testament, 'the Alpha and the Omega, the first and the last, the beginning and the end' (Revelation 22:13). He is, to cite Charles Haddon Spurgeon, 'the sum and substance of the gospel, who is in himself all theology, the incarnation of every precious truth, the all-glorious embodiment of the way, the truth and the life' (Robert Backhouse, ed., *The Autobiography of C.H. Spurgeon*, Hodder & Stoughton, 1993, p. 186). This book seeks to set out the fullness of his being, the A to Z of both his eternal and his earthly 'careers'. It is written in the belief that we need the whole Christ, not just a partial Christ who might serve us, for instance, by way of example for living, or atoning sacrifice, or exalted recipient of our worship. We need to know and love the whole Christ and to work out in our own discipleship the full implications of every aspect of his being. If it is possible to have a God who is too small, as it surely is, it is equally possible to have a small Christ. A small Christ makes us, in turn, people of limited imagination and breadth. Nothing but a large vision of a great Lord will do, and these studies are devoted to that end.

I have chosen to avoid direct quotations from other sources as much as possible; however, as I have used it quite fully, I do wish to acknowledge my source for the excellent quotation from Kierkegaard on page 80, which I owe to Bishop John Saxbee in the Introduction to *Reading the Bible: Approaching and Understanding Scripture* (SCM, 2006). The prayer with which this book ends is taken from the Advent Order for Communion of *The Methodist Worship Book* (Methodist Publishing House, 1999).

Note: Rather than including the full Bible passage every day, I have taken a 'key verse' approach. While it will be very helpful, though not essential, to read the designated passage in full, the day's 'key verse' will be the focus for my comment. In line with the book's aim of delving deeper into the teaching behind the text, I will sometimes spend more than one day reflecting on the same 'key verse'.

Part One

A journey of discovery

(1) Ash Wednesday

Christ the key to all things

READ JOHN 1:1–18

And the Word became flesh and lived among us, and we have seen his glory, the glory as of a father's only son, full of grace and truth (v. 14).

A few years ago, I was a speaker at Easter People, the Bible Week initiated by the late Rob Frost. The organisers decided to put me in the alternative venue, where the idea was to do things differently, with more of a performing arts emphasis. The brains behind this venue came up with a new idea. On stage they erected a Christmas tree made of coat hangers. Every speaker was supposed to suspend something from the tree and then talk about it for a full minute without hesitation, deviation or repetition. This was fine, except that they forgot to tell the speakers that this was going to happen. So there we were, scrabbling around in our baggage for something to hang from the tree.

The speaker before me was Adrian Plass, who hung up his toothbrush. I have forgotten now what exactly he said about it, but I do remember the toothbrush. Then it was my turn.

All I had with me was a bunch of car keys. Inspiration struck: Jesus Christ is the key that unlocks the mysteries of the universe. That, it seems to me, is the great theme that runs through these magnificent first 18 verses of John's Gospel, which are sometimes called the 'Prologue' to John's Gospel. That astonishing belief in Jesus, it equally seems to me, is what lies at the very heart of the Christian faith.

Today we begin a journey together. We do so on a day that marks the beginning of a pilgrimage Christians take every year, at least in their minds—a journey to Jerusalem, to the cross and to the empty tomb of Jesus. The purpose of our journey is to understand how Christ can be the key to the mysteries of the universe. We shall do this by recalling who Christ is and the journey that he has first made towards us, which precedes any journey that we can make towards him. It is a journey from eternity into time and then from time into eternity. In the church's language, we sometimes speak of God's 'prevenient grace'. By this we mean that Christianity is not, first and foremost, a religion that tells of how we can reach up to God but one that speaks of how God has reached down to us. God has gone before us, coming to us in love and grace in order that we might find him as he draws near. If we ever reach out to God and seek him, it is because his love first prompts us and enables us to do so. Salvation is of the Lord. It comes as a gracious gift from God, as does everything that is good, true and beautiful.

What does it mean for Christ to unlock the mysteries of the universe? The greatest mystery is the mystery of God himself. How can finite and sinful human beings speak of God? God is infinitely great, greater than the universe itself, in which there are said to be ten billion galaxies, each containing ten billion stars. By comparison with them, we are so small and insignificant. Our minds and imaginations are all the more puny by contrast with the God who exceeds them all. We might as well seek to contain the oceans in a bucket. We cannot speak of God because, on our own, we have no way of knowing God, no way of unlocking the mystery of God's own being. But there is a key to that mystery and it is Jesus Christ, the one who appears in John's Gospel as 'the Word of God'. 'In the beginning was the Word, and the Word was with God, and the Word was God' (1:1). 'The Word became flesh and lived among us, and we have seen his glory' (v. 14). This is how the Christian can begin to speak of God, because God has first of all spoken to us in a Son who has come to us, clothed in our flesh and living our life.

Jesus is the Word of God. What do we use words for? One way we use them is to express ourselves. Every speaker—perhaps every singer, too—knows that there is something very satisfying about expressing yourself. If Jesus Christ is the Word of God, we can say that in him God is expressing himself; that what is within this mysterious God, who is behind and beyond all things, finds expression in Jesus Christ the Son of God. The Word of God is God's self-expression. We might say that he is the very image of the Father (Colossians 1:15).

That leads us to another thing about words: they communicate. They take what is in my mind and heart and communicate it into yours. If Jesus Christ is the Word of God, he is God communicating God's own self, in order to unlock the mystery of who he is. Because Christ is God's Son, we know that there is a Father, of whom Christ is the image and likeness, a Father who wants to penetrate the darkness and make himself known to us. In Jesus Christ we see the Father.

Those who have seen the Son have seen the Father (John 14:9). Jesus Christ is the Word of the Father. In Jesus, the invisible is made visible. Notice again the words: 'The Word became flesh and lived among us.' In Jesus Christ, the language of eternity is translated into the language of time. God's eternal Word becomes flesh and is clothed in the kind of humanity that you and I can recognise and understand. We cannot speak God's language, so God comes to us speaking in our own. Jesus Christ is the great translator and the great translation of the living God, God's cross-cultural communication. For this reason John goes on to say, in today's passage, 'No one has ever seen God. It is God the only Son, who is close to the Father's heart, who has made him known' (v. 18). This is why we can say that he is the key that unlocks the secrets of God. This is why we should listen to him. This is where our journey must begin.

(2) Thursday

The Christ who is eternal

READ JOHN 1:1–18

---

*In the beginning was the Word, and the Word was
with God, and the Word was God. He was in the
beginning with God (vv. 1–2).*

Our first journey is the journey of discovery. We are seeking
to understand who Christ is in his fullness, in order that we
may be fully devoted to him. If Christ is the key that unlocks
the mystery of God's own being, this can only be because
there is a way in which he shares God's being as God.
According to our key verse, this means that he was 'in the
beginning with God', and he 'was God'. We have to debate
what this means. To be with God 'in the beginning' surely
refers to the beginning of creation (Genesis 1:1). When
space and time were summoned into being, the Word was
already there, preceding it all. He was preceding it all because
whatever God is, the Word also was. As we saw in yesterday's
reading, John asserts that the Word who 'was' then 'became'
flesh (v. 14). Something momentous and world-transforming
happened: Christ became something he had not previously

been—a part of the creation, sharing creation's finite limits and vulnerability, which is what 'flesh' implies.

Before we can make journeys of discovery or devotion, we need to see that Christ has first made his own journey from eternity into time. This clearly marks him out from any other human being. Human lives begin when they are conceived in the womb, but Christ is different. Christ 'was' before ever he was conceived in the womb. In the human being known as Jesus of Nazareth, the Word of God—who has been from the beginning, from eternity, who was with God and was God— has found expression and become incarnate. This means that the Word of God pre-existed the human person called Jesus of Nazareth, became identical with him in the incarnation and in this way became the Christ of God, who is God's saving gift to us.

In all of this, there is certainly a great deal that needs to be understood! Although, for many of us, these may be familiar truths, they can never stop being utterly astonishing ones. To say that Christ shares in eternity turns out to be a matter of the utmost importance. There are those who have tried to explain the importance of Jesus by saying that he was a human being especially favoured by God, even one who had been adopted by God to share in a special divine status. Others have thought that Jesus was created by God as the first and highest of God's works, a kind of angelic or semi-divine figure (although to be 'semi' divine would seem to be a contradiction in terms). But none of these attempts to honour Jesus really work. They succeed only in making Jesus less than the one he actually is, for underlying these apparently difficult patterns of thought there is one massive existential question: is Jesus Christ a human being to be revered and honoured only, or is the Word of God manifest in the flesh to be *worshipped*?

According to the Hebrew Scriptures, which Christians accept as the Old Testament, there is only one God, and that one God alone is to be worshipped (Deuteronomy 5:7; 6: 4–5). To worship Christ, if he did not share in the divine being, would be wrong. It might be quite proper to honour and revere him, but certainly not to bow before him in worship, to call him 'my Lord and my God' (John 20:28) and give him divine honour and praise. Yet this is exactly what we find that the first Christians did, and this is what the visions of the book of Revelation inspire Christians of all generations to do. Here, the Lamb of God (who is also the Word of God known as Jesus Christ) shares both the throne of God and the worship of God as 'every creature in heaven and on earth and under the earth and in the sea' says, 'To the one seated on the throne and to the Lamb be blessing and honour and glory and might for ever and ever!' (Revelation 5:13).

The eternity of Christ is actually a quality associated with his deity, his sharing in the divine nature. It turns out to be a key assertion about the person of Christ. God is eternal; Christ is God; therefore Christ shares in eternity. To put it the other way round, Christ is eternal; eternity is a quality of God; therefore Christ is God. To make this claim is not abstract theology but a statement about something that is of the greatest importance to Christians and must be allowed to shape their lives. As we have already noted, without this statement it would not be appropriate for Christians to worship Christ. Yet this is exactly what they do whenever they pronounce the Gloria: 'Glory to the Father, and to the Son, and to the Holy Spirit, as it was in the beginning, is now and shall be for ever. Amen.'

Jesus Christ is the key that unlocks the mystery of God. We can add to that another belief: because he unlocks the mystery of God, he is also able to unlock the mystery of our own lives. He enables us to see ourselves within the framework of ultimate reality or of eternity. It is out of the mystery of eternity that Christ has come, giving a meaning to time. Everybody lives for something. The most thoughtful people know what they most value. It has been said that, strictly speaking, there is no such thing as a 'godless' man or woman. Everybody has something that they regard as their object of ultimate devotion, even if it may not be worthy of the name. It is important that whatever we live for is really worth the love and devotion we bring to it; otherwise we ourselves become diminished. We come to resemble whatever it is that we most honour. For Christians, to honour Christ is to root ourselves in someone who is of eternal value and significance, someone who is worthy, and that can only do us good.

(3) Friday

Before Abraham was, I am

READ JOHN 8:39–59

Jesus said to them, 'Very truly, I tell you, before Abraham was, I am' (v. 58).

It seems as though it was not always easy to have Jesus around. He had a definite point of view and was prepared to press it home. Often we find him disputing with those of his generation, especially with the Pharisees. In all likelihood, Jesus had more in common with the Pharisees than with many others of his contemporaries, but sometimes it is the people we are closest to with whom we argue most. Mind you, Jesus had to put up with plenty of abuse. In this chapter he is accused of being a demon-possessed Samaritan (v. 48), which must have ranked as a ripe insult of the highest order. Quite the opposite was the case: Jesus was consumed with a passion for the God of Israel, whose glory he sought (v. 50). His opponents were vitriolic because Jesus was attacking their self-esteem, questioning whether they really were children of Abraham or even children of God (vv. 39, 42). If they were either of these things, they would have recognised that Jesus himself had come from God.

The bedrock of Jesus' life was this sense of profound communion with the Father (v. 55). Whatever else we may wish to say about Jesus, believer and unbeliever must agree that Jesus felt himself to be in an intimate relationship with God, like that of a beloved son with a loving father. This gave him an extraordinary self-belief when it came to interpreting God's will, so much so that his opponents asked him caustically whether he considered himself greater than Abraham, the very founder of their faith and their nation (v. 53). This set Jesus off in a surprising direction, making the claim that Abraham himself anticipated the day of Jesus' coming and rejoiced as he did so. Perhaps he had in mind the promise made to Abraham that the whole world would be blessed through Abraham's descendants (Genesis 12:3) and the assurance, when Isaac was born, that the promised posterity would indeed come to be (Genesis 21:1, 12). At any rate, to picture Abraham as subordinate to Jesus was like a red rag to a bull as far as Jesus' opponents were concerned, and understandably so. Was this a deluded would-be messiah on an ego trip, they may have asked. Jesus made it worse before it got better, saying, 'Very truly, I tell you, before Abraham was, I am.'

The opponents' response to Jesus was to pick up stones with which to obliterate him. These words were considered blasphemous, an insult to the name of God and a claim to the kind of status that only imposters thought themselves to have. This Jesus must be either bad or mad. In this one short sentence he had claimed enormous significance for himself, associating himself with the God of Israel by using the implied title 'I am', which was the sacred name of the Most High revealed to Moses at the burning bush:

But Moses said to God, 'If I come to the Israelites and say to them, "The God of your ancestors has sent me to you", and they ask me, "What is his name?" what shall I say to them?' God said to Moses, 'I AM WHO I AM.' He said further, 'Thus shall you say to the Israelites, "I AM has sent me to you."'' (Exodus 3:13–14)

Here on the lips of Jesus are words that claim divine identity. Jesus regarded himself as in some way sharing in the everlasting life of God, such that he was before Abraham was: he existed before the patriarchs existed, transcending the limits of time and space.

Jesus could say these things only because he knew himself to be in a relationship of intimate communion with the Father, which meant that he participated decisively in the divine life. It is surely wrong and unhelpful for us to imagine that Jesus went round with the words of the Nicene Creed ('God from God, Light from Light, True God from True God') ringing in his ears. The doctrines of the Trinity and the pre-existence of the Son of God belong to the Church's later attempts to capture the mystery of Christ's identity and the real Christian experience of him as the mediator between God and humanity. But the later formulations are rooted in words such as these, found in John's inspired interpretation of Jesus. John's interpretation, in its turn, is rooted in Christ's own earthly knowledge and John's close experience of the one he encountered and knew personally: 'We declare to you what was from the beginning, what we have heard, what we have seen with our eyes, what we have looked at and touched with our hands, concerning the word of life' (1 John 1:1).

Jesus' words, and the claims they contain, are astonishing. Like the Jewish believers who first heard them, we are at liberty not to believe them. They clearly incited some people to anger and disbelief and to the assertion that such claims were impossible. They even made people want to throw stones at Jesus. We must readily agree that were anybody else to utter words of this kind, we would reject them. Yet the truth is astonishing. Christian believers have staked their life on the belief that these words are true and that they are life-transforming. They are believed to be true because they are congruent with what we know of the life, teaching, death and resurrection of Jesus Christ, which are understood to be the actions of the living God who comes among us to seek and save the lost, to redeem a world that has gone astray. This is how Christians see Jesus—as the revelation in time of a wise and good purpose that has existed from before the creation of the world and has been put into effect in his life and career. Jesus is our glimpse into the final reality, ultimate meaning and deep purpose of all things.

(4) Saturday

The Christ who accompanied Israel

READ 1 CORINTHIANS 10:1–13

For they drank from the spiritual rock that followed them, and the rock was Christ (v. 4).

When reading the Bible, it is possible to get the wrong impression. Inevitably, we read scripture chronologically, beginning with creation and the story of Israel, progressing into the Gospels and then moving on to the story of the Church. As the Bible is God's story, we encounter the unfolding revelation of God's own being and nature as we read. First we have the God of Israel, who elects and forms a people for himself. Arising from this story is an encounter with the Messiah, Jesus, 'the Son of the Most High' (Luke 1:32), who makes his appearance as an earthly and historical figure in the Gospels. He is Emmanuel, 'God with us' (Matthew 1:23). Then we move into the realm of the Spirit, who is poured out on the day of Pentecost and is the continuing presence of Christ among those who acknowledge him. The

Spirit is God 'even more with us', because the Spirit is not restricted by space or limitation. Out of this unfolding story, Christians came to see God as the relational triune God who is Creator, Redeemer and Transformer.

So where might we gain the wrong impression? By following the flow of biblical narrative, we might infer that the Son of God 'came into being' with the Gospels or that the Spirit was non-existent until the day of Pentecost. In fact, one verse might be read as implying just that: 'Now (Jesus) said this about the Spirit, which believers in him were to receive; for as yet there was no Spirit' (John 7:39). What this means, of course, is that the age of the Spirit that began with the day of Pentecost had yet to come. But if the Son and the Spirit are divine persons within the communion of the one triune God, they do not come into existence at a certain point. They might be revealed in time as the history of salvation unfolds, but they have always been, not only 'before Abraham' but from all eternity. The triune God is the everlasting God, without beginning and without end.

If we read the Bible not chronologically but from back to front, in the light of all we know of God by the end of the Bible, we will understand it differently. The one whom we call 'Christ' and the reality we designate 'Spirit' are not late comers to the story but are present and active from the beginning, although in forms hidden and sometimes disguised from our sight.

To quote St Augustine, 'In the Old Testament the New is concealed, and in the New the Old is revealed.' It is something like this that Paul has in mind in today's passage. He invites his readers to look back over the history of Israel, especially the time of Israel's wanderings in the wilderness, and to find the one whom we call Christ already present there. At one point in Israel's wandering, at a place called Meribah, they were badly in need of water and an insurrection was being threatened. Moses was told to strike a nearby rock, from which abundant water then began to flow (Numbers 20:1–13). This rock, says Paul, was Christ. Now this cannot literally be true, so what did Paul mean? He was spiritualising the meaning of the events described in Numbers as a way of instructing the Christians to whom he was writing about the continuing life and refreshment that is in Christ the Saviour. At the same time, he was calling our attention to the fact that even under the old covenant it was Christ who was the mediator of salvation. Christ did not begin to be that mediator only after his incarnation but had, from the beginning, been the means through which God drew near to human beings, reconciling them to God's own self.

We might say that in the events of the earthly and historical life, death and resurrection of Jesus, God was revealing and enacting in time that which God is able to do and does do from eternity. Because this is so, we are entitled to see Christ everywhere in the Hebrew Scriptures, even though he was not known there in these terms and by this name.

In later readings, we will go on to see other ways in which the triune God's activity is glimpsed in those Hebrew Scriptures. How might these insights shape the way we read the Bible? It should first be said that it is not right to force a meaning on any part of the Bible. We must let the scriptures be what they are, seeking to grasp (as far as we can) how they would have been understood when they were first written and heard. Let us not be too keen to impose a meaning on them that could never have been imagined at the time. When we have done this with integrity, however, we should also see that each part of the biblical story belongs within a book that accumulates meaning as the story unfolds further. Old scriptures take on new significance in a changed context.

The idea of the exodus, for instance, developed in the New Testament to refer not only to the people of Israel being set free from the bondage of Egypt, but to all people being set free from the bondage of sin and evil. Liberation and freedom are God's gifts to us in Christ. If this is so now, under the new covenant celebrated by Christians, it must have been through Christ, as the great mediator of salvation, that these gifts were given to Israel under the old covenant.

When preachers preach from the Hebrew Scriptures (which they should and must do), the greatest challenge is always to take that extra step of interpretation and show how the ideas beginning to unfold there can point us to the Christ who is the centre of faith. As Jesus himself said to the eager Bible students of his day, 'You search the scriptures because you think that in them you have eternal life; and it is they that testify on my behalf. Yet you refuse to come to me to have life' (John 5:39–40). Neither Bible reading nor Bible study are complete until we have done just this.

(5) *First Sunday*

Christ the Creator

READ COLOSSIANS 1:15–23

For in him all things in heaven and on earth were created, things visible and invisible, whether thrones or dominions or rulers or powers—all things have been created through him and for him (v. 16).

We have already noted that Christ did not come into being at the point when he was conceived but had already existed 'from the beginning'. For this reason it is possible to discern the presence of the Son of God in the history of Israel before his incarnation. Although there was a point when he became flesh, the Son of God has been with the Father from before all time (John 1:1–2, 14). To find Christ present in the story of Israel is therefore not enough. We need to discern his presence in the very work of creation.

It is amazing to see how quickly and decisively the writers of the New Testament went on to draw this conclusion. It is clearly stated in today's passage. Through Christ, everything that is has come into being, all that we can see and all that is beyond our sight. They exist by him and for him. A similar claim is made in other places: John 1:3 says, 'All things came into being through him, and without him not one thing came into being.' This verse is particularly interesting since it sets the Word of God (whom we know as Christ) apart from the whole of creation. If all things came into being through him, then he existed prior to and apart from all created things. He could not have been the means of his own creation, and that means, in the words of the Nicene Creed, that he was 'begotten not made'. In time, the Word of God was to become flesh and so also become part of the created order, without ceasing to be who and what he had always been. This is a highly distinctive aspect of Christian faith. If we remove the idea of Christ's pre-existence from the web of Christian belief, we call into question everything that follows from it and reduce Christ to a mere creature.

Another verse that confirms this understanding of Christ is Hebrews 1:2, which, among other things, asserts that it is through the Son that God 'created the worlds'. True, then, to the insight by which we have found the presence of Christ in the story of Israel, we can now find him in the very beginning of the Bible and in the beginning of creation itself. Genesis 1 pictures the creative work of God as the product of God's speaking: God created by his powerful word. All God has to do is speak and things happen. The word of God is much the same thing as the act of God, since, when God speaks, there is a response. So, in the creation narrative of Genesis 1, we are told repeatedly that 'God said' and it was. John 1, which closely echoes Genesis 1, identifies the Word with Christ, and so we may conclude that through the Word, through God's agent whom we now acknowledge as Christ, the worlds came into being in the first place.

This is a stupendous claim. Indeed, so stupendous is it that we are left wondering how the first Christian thinkers and writers arrived at it (always acknowledging the help of God's revealing Spirit, of course). A sceptic might simply see it as a vast overstatement, something that could never be attributed to any human being anywhere. But perhaps the first Christian witnesses grasped that the saving work they had experienced through Christ was a gift of God, a gift of new creation, and that Christ was its agent. This could have led them to work backwards and ascribe the act of first creation to God, through Christ as his original agent. It would then be consistent to say that the one through whom the world was made in the first place became incarnate to repair and redeem a world gone wrong, in a new act of divine creation, brought about this time not by the speaking of a word but by the costly offering of a life.

Alternatively, it may be that they understood a thing or two about God's wisdom. Proverbs 8:22–31 expands on this theme at length, describing the wisdom that was with God in the beginning, by means of which God created the world. This wisdom had now appeared in Christ to bring salvation to those who believe. One significant difference here is that Proverbs 8:22 speaks of God 'creating' wisdom as the first of his acts, and this could be thought to conflict with what we have seen in John 1:3 (although there are other possible translations, and we should ask whether God 'creates' wisdom or already 'possesses' it?). Apart from this, though, in other places Jesus is described as 'wisdom from God' (1 Corinthians 1:30). Christ is the incarnation of the same divine wisdom by which God created the world in the first place. This means that in Christ, as the Saviour, we not only have insight into the salvation of the human race but are able to have insight into the very depths of creation itself.

There is an immediate application of this belief. To be a follower of Christ makes us more 'worldly'. If the world is

Christ's, made through him and for him, faithful Christians should care about and care for what belongs to him. The creation, with its layers of mineral, vegetable, animal and human realities, does not revolve around the human species in general or individual persons in particular. It revolves around the Christ who is its source. There are many good reasons for nurturing and protecting a planet threatened by global warming and pollution, but this is the best of all. Being 'green' is not a dispensable option for disciples but a direct implication of our commitment to the Son of God and our respect for everything that he has called into being.

(6) Monday

The Christ who defines creation

READ COLOSSIANS 1:15–23

For in him all things in heaven and on earth were created, things visible and invisible, whether thrones or dominions or rulers or powers—all things have been created through him and for him (v. 16).

Before we move on from this passage and this key text, there are other aspects of it that we would do well to note. If it is through Christ that the worlds have been made, and if it is for him that they exist in the first place, then there is something to be said about the underlying nature and purpose of creation. Christ is the revelation of that purpose. Some years ago, the eminent professor and cosmologist Stephen Hawking was Sue Lawley's guest on *Desert Island Discs*. Towards the end of the programme Sue Lawley asked him the inevitable question: 'With all your great knowledge about the origins of the universe, where in your thinking is there any room for God?' Professor Hawking replied, 'Science can answer many questions, but there is one question that science will never be able to answer, and that is why there is something and not nothing.'

Philosophers might debate whether this is an intelligible question, at least in the form in which it is posed. Is it possible to ask whether 'nothing' can or cannot be? Nothing is, after all, nothing. But the question can be asked in other ways. Why does anything that exists actually exist? Even if we uncover the processes by which things have come to be and explain everything about the 'how', we have still not addressed the 'why'. Therefore, in one sense, we have 'explained' nothing at all. We have simply moved to another level of questions. But once we say that all things have been made through and for Christ, we have entered into new territory. We are now asking theological questions about the nature and purpose of existence and claiming that these aspects of existence are bound up with Christ. If Christ is the key that unlocks the mystery of God, he is also the key that unlocks the mystery of creation. He makes it intelligible to us. Creation has been called into being so that it may learn how to respond to God in the same full and complete way that Christ responded. Only in this way can the creation, and human beings within it, discover the fullness of its potential and finally become what it is called to be. Creation has been made not for the chaos and discord that too often characterise it but for communion with God, like the communion that Christ enjoys with the Father. It should be noted that, in this chapter of Colossians, Christ is understood to be the one not only through whom all things have been made but through whom they will one day be fully reconciled. All of this has been accomplished through the cross, which has a universal impact (v. 20). Christ is the hope for the healing of creation as well as for the reconciliation of human beings.

In the Prologue to John's Gospel that we read on Ash Wednesday, the Gospel writer drew upon the background of Hebrew thought, in which God's creative word was believed to be powerful. This creative word could be seen in Christ, through whom the worlds have been made. By drawing also upon a background of Greek thought, the writer weaves in another idea, concerning the Logos. Christ is the Logos, and the Logos (also meaning 'word') was understood in Greek philosophy to be the intelligence behind the creation, the principle of intelligibility hidden beneath the surface of the visible world. Christ is therefore understood to be the one who first gave meaning to the world and then revealed in his incarnation what that meaning was. Christ was not, therefore, some kind of visitor to this world but was at its heart, as much in its depths as in its heights.

Pursue whatever form of human enquiry you will, whether in music or science, art or philosophy, and it is possible to meet Christ there, in the beauty, the rhythms and the stability of creation in all its varying aspects. In one sense, therefore, Christians are the most worldly of people. They do not believe in the kind of religion that takes them out of the real, physical universe into some abstract form of piety or escape or world denial, in order to find God. They are confident that they can immerse themselves in the stuff of worldly reality, in its daily rhythms and demands, and remain close to Christ. They are certainly entitled to be disillusioned and disturbed by many of the ways in which this world shows itself not yet to be in communion with God, but they know that, beneath this, the grain of the universe is shaped and patterned by the Christ through whom it has been created.

It has been said that there is not one part of the world in which Christ does not place his foot and say, 'Mine!' This should not be understood in an imperialistic way, as though

Christ (or Christians in his name) is eager for world domination and global power. It should be understood, rather, that God in Christ cares for and is concerned about every aspect of life, and that he is about the business of wooing it back to himself. Only when every aspect of the world resonates in harmony with Christ will it come to fullness of life. Pivotal in this transforming work are human beings, who have been given a role of stewardship within the creation, a role that reflects God's own nurturing sovereignty. The well-being of the creation is bound up with the behaviour of humans, who have the power to vandalise the peace of the creation, and have done so with conspicuous success. But when people are reconciled to Christ and find their life in him, they become, with Christ, part of 'the beginning, the firstborn from the dead' (Colossians 1:18) in preparing the way for the eventual reconciliation of all things to the Father through Christ. To be 'in Christ' is to come close to the beating heart of the universe, to get in touch with its fundamental reason for being and to become part of God's purpose of completing and fulfilling it—a purpose that has been intended from the beginning.

(7) Tuesday

The Christ who upholds creation

READ HEBREWS 1

He is the reflection of God's glory and the exact imprint of God's very being, and he sustains all things by his powerful word (v. 3).

This key verse will claim our attention for two days: today we will reflect on its second part and tomorrow we will consider its first part. In many ways, the idea that Christ 'sustains all things by his powerful word' follows on from what we have learnt about Christ as creator and as the one who gives pattern and shape to creation. It is not as though the triune God, having called the worlds into being through the Word, then neglects and ignores them. Quite the contrary: the continuing existence of the creation is dependent moment by moment upon Christ and his word of power, as he continues to speak creatively into the universe and to guard all things from collapsing into chaos and dissolution.

The expression 'all things' is found here, and is also often to be found in the writings of Paul. It is clear enough that 'all things' does not leave anything out. Everything we can

34

possibly imagine continues to receive moment-by-moment attention from the Lord of all. God is not restricted to parts of the creation, as if there were no-go zones for the Creator. Even though the world and its human creatures may exist in alienation from God, this God 'makes his sun rise on the evil and on the good, and sends rain on the righteous and on the unrighteous' (Matthew 5:45), and does so persistently, faithfully and kindly. God creates and preserves what has been summoned into being because 'his compassion is over all that he has made' (Psalm 145:9).

The fact that the creation has to be upheld rather suggests that it is under some form of threat, the threat of collapse back into the chaos and non-being out of which it came. It needs to be sustained against this threat, its durability and sustainability being maintained so that creation may have space and time within which to be. Into the notion of God's creative activity comes, therefore, the idea that God is acting through Christ to save the world, to set it in order and overcome the chaos that might engulf it. This idea helps us to make a link between the role of the eternal Word in sustaining all things and the work of the incarnate Word in being its Saviour. To put the question bluntly, if the Word became flesh, does this mean that he then took leave of absence from holding the universe together; and, if so, who was 'minding the shop' when this happened? In response we might say that although the incarnate Word, Christ, was wholly the Word of God, he was not the whole of the Word of God. Within the divine freedom, it is within God's power to be both eternally active and present in time simultaneously, entirely without contradiction.

To recognise that Christ is eternally preserving the world from the threat of non-being enables us to see how his incarnate work is both continuous with and an extension of his eternal work. By entering into time and becoming a particular human being, he reveals God's infinite resourcefulness in overcoming the problem of human sin and alienation. His life, death and resurrection are all part of the work of upholding creation and ensuring that the good work God has begun in creation is not derailed or diverted by human sinfulness. Rather, the God who has purposed to bring all things into unity with himself, and to ensure that creation's goal is finally reached, does this both in eternity and time through the same agent, who is his own Son.

The word 'God' is capable of a broad range of meanings and is used in human discourse to capture a whole variety of concepts. For some, the word is used simply to mean the sum total of all things. For others, God is a necessary philosophical construct, a way of accounting for the origins of things. So they may believe that God made the world but left it thereafter to its own devices. For yet others, God is the unnameable and impersonal power that undergirds everything and is best thought of as infinite energy or unfathomable depth: to name or understand this power as personal would be to trivialise it.

There might be lessons to learn from some of these points of view, but none of them matches fully the Christian concept. For Christians, God is other than the world. If the world were to be taken away, God would still be, because God's existence is not a product of the world, but the world is a product of God's existence. This God continues to be intimately involved with the creation, to grant it graciously every fresh moment and every new breath. Although God is greatly to be exalted, God is not distant but close to us. God is in the depths as well as in the heights. Most of all, this Christian God is fully and intensely personal—someone and not just something—although it should also be added that our human personhood is no more than a flickering image of

God's full and complete personhood. God is not just another being, like the rest of us, but the ground, source and origin of all being. In this sense, God is indeed unfathomable and any language we use to speak of God runs the danger of diminishing the greatness of God. But to think that this God 'upholds' us is a humbling and ennobling thought.

Human beings are given freedom and responsibility by their Creator and are called into partnership with God's own self in the work of creation. They may and do, tragically, misuse their freedom, but the gracious love of God is shown in that rather than withdrawing the right to life from us, as we might deserve, the God revealed in Jesus Christ continues to give us space and time in which to live. Even more than this, God has acted in Christ to preserve us from ourselves, to show how we may be restored to communion with God's self, so that we, with all creation, may come to our proper goal in a restored and reconciled universe.

(8) Wednesday

The Christ who is God's image

READ HEBREWS 1

---

*He is the reflection of God's glory and the exact
imprint of God's very being, and he sustains all
things by his powerful word (v. 3).*

Our focus today is on the first part of this key text: Christ is
the image of God. If we have followed the train of thought
outlined so far, the divine identity of Christ should be
reasonably clear. Christians see in the human being Jesus
Christ one who already existed before his birth and whose
origin is before all time, in and with the Creator of the
universe, whom we are able to imagine through Christ as
'Father'. Both in eternity and through his incarnation in time,
Christ is revealed as the very image of God, the expression of
the very nature of the living God. To 'see' Christ is to see God
in Christ and to understand both that there is no other God
and that God is no other than what we see in him. In John
14:8–11, one of Jesus' disciples, Philip, is depicted as saying
to him, 'Lord, show us the Father and we will be satisfied.'
Jesus responds, 'Have I been with you all this time, Philip,

and you still do not know me? Whoever has seen me has seen the Father... Believe me that I am in the Father and the Father is in me.' Christ is the clearest depiction of God we are ever likely to find.

Today's key verse captures this thought in the idea that just as a coin carries the impression of the monarch's head, so Christ bears the image of the Father. It has been rightly claimed that the greatest truth for our times is not the divinity of the Christ, great though that undoubtedly is, but the Christ-likeness of the divinity. These truths must, in fact, be seen as two sides of one coin: because Christ is truly God, he is able to represent the Father accurately and without distortion; and because we see God truly in him, we can be assured as to what God is like. There is deep reassurance in these words. People carry around in their heads many different ideas and images of God, which can sometimes be frightening and unhelpful. If their primary image of God is as a punitive and vengeful deity, it is not surprising if people decide, sooner or later, that they no longer wish to believe in such a God.

Cardinal Basil Hume once told a story from his own experience. As a child, he was educated partly by nuns. On one occasion he took a sweet from the tin without permission and was told by a sister, 'Basil, when you took that sweet, God was watching you.' This affected the way he thought about God for some time: it made him imagine God as one who disapproves. Later he came to realise that God had indeed been watching him when he took the sweet, but was probably saying, 'Go on, take two!' To see God accurately portrayed in Christ is to be set free from oppressive and destructive alternatives that make it hard to relate to God: if God is the Christ-like God, we are encouraged to draw near.

In the story of Israel there are continual warnings against

making idols and bowing down to them; in fact, the first of the Ten Commandments is devoted to this theme (Exodus 20:4; see also Isaiah 44:9–20). Idols made by human hands can never do justice to the God of Israel, who is beyond our capacity to portray. Indeed, when we worship idols we not only show disrespect to the living God but we also dehumanise ourselves, since we have a tendency to become like whatever we worship (Psalm 115:3–8). The only image of God that is considered acceptable within the created sphere is the image of God within humanity, since 'God created humankind in his own image, in the image of God he created them; male and female he created them' (Genesis 1:27). If human beings have the capacity to be in the image of God, it is tragically the case that, in reality, they have lost much of their likeness to God. They are like a mirror that, if turned towards an object, faithfully reflects it but, once turned away, does not do so. If turned back to the object, the mirror may reflect it again; and, in the same way, when we turn back to God we may indeed come to resemble God as we should. However, there is one who is in the image of God, who bears the Father's likeness, 'and we have seen his glory, the glory as of a father's only son, full of grace and truth' (John 1:14). He is also the means by which we can turn to God, so that we also may reflect him.

In the next chapter of Hebrews, the author refers back to Psalm 8, which speaks of human beings in very positive terms: 'What are human beings that you are mindful of them, or mortals, that you care for them? You have made them only a little lower than the angels; you have crowned them with glory and honour, subjecting all things under their feet' (Hebrews 2:6–8a). The writer of Hebrews goes on to acknowledge that this noble vision has not been fulfilled, except in Christ: 'As it is, we do not yet see everything in subjection to them, but we do see Jesus, who for a little while was made lower than the angels, now crowned with glory and honour because of the suffering of death' (vv. 8b–9). Jesus is the great sign of hope for humanity because in him the image of God has been restored. Being the image of God from eternity, he came to spell out this image in terms of a particular human life and destiny, even one that involved suffering and death. This is what the God of holy love looks like: self-giving, self-offering sacrifice; generous, gracious, outpoured love; holy, uncompromising compassion. To be able to believe that this is what God is like, that this is the nature of ultimate reality, is good news. At the beating heart of all creation is not uncaring emptiness but warm, passionate love.

(9) Thursday

The Christ who humbled himself

READ PHILIPPIANS 2:1–8

---

*Let the same mind be in you that was in Christ
Jesus, who, though he was in the form of God, did
not regard equality with God as something to be
exploited, but emptied himself, taking the form of a
slave, being born in human likeness (vv. 5–7).*

Although, until this point, we have been following the
journey of Jesus Christ in his pre-existence, it has been hard
not to refer continually to his incarnation. It is only through
the incarnation that we have any understanding of Christ at
all. However, our focus now moves decisively to the journey
from eternity into time. Philippians 2 is one of the passages
that speaks clearly of this journey and is deservedly well-
known. Scholars speak of these verses as a 'hymn', in the
belief that, along with other New Testament passages, they
represent one of those terse summaries of Christian teaching
that were circulated in the early Church, to be memorised by
the believers as part of their basic education in the faith. Paul
is able therefore to refer to them as part of what every disciple

would be expected to know—the commonly owned doctrine of the churches.

There are two levels at which this passage might helpfully be understood. At the higher level, it is an account of the self-humbling of the Son of God, who left behind the glory and richness of the divine presence in order to share in the human condition. Although he was in the form of God, sharing in God's nature and divine honour, he emptied himself and was born in human likeness. As a human being he lived humbly and was obedient to the Father's will, even though it led to death upon a cross. It was not that the Father willed him to suffer simply for the sake of suffering, as though suffering were somehow glorious. Rather, the Father willed to identify so fully with humankind, in his Son, that he would inevitably endure the suffering that the human condition entails. More than this, because the Son came to give himself for others, his particular destiny involved the way of the cross. This is a cosmic drama since it is about God being made incarnate as a human being. We see a particular gospel shape in this passage as the Son of God enters humbly into time and then returns gloriously to the Father, having accomplished the work he came to do.

At another level, this passage should be read in parallel with the account of Adam and Eve, which defines for us the human condition. Human beings were created in the 'form' of God in that they were made to be in God's image. Rather than humbly accepting their finite but noble place in dependence upon God, however, they have grasped at equality with God. They have believed the lie that by disregarding the word of God and choosing a forbidden alternative, they would be 'like God, knowing good and evil' (Genesis 3:5). This is an attempt to displace God, to dethrone the Creator and insert ourselves into the place of divinity by self-exaltation. Human beings, who have no right to such a place, have attempted to acquire it, thus bringing themselves into personal and corporate ruin. By contrast, the Son of God, who has every right to the highest place of dignity, has emptied himself in humility and given himself over to suffering for the sake of others. In this way, the saving God contradicted the human contradiction of God's own self and redeemed us.

There are few teachings more radical than the belief that the God who is the source of all things entered into time and became part of the created order, without ceasing to be who and what he had always been. This is exactly what the Christian faith claims about Jesus and it involves an acknowledgment of the humility of God. Other religious traditions may find this very thought offensive, a stumbling-block to their assumptions about the greatness of God (1 Corinthians 1:22–24). They might believe in a God who would never consent to die on a cross. For Christians, though, the glory of God consists in large measure in what others might find offensive, in the very idea that the great and transcendent God, the ruler of the universe, is willing for love of the creation to embrace humility, self-emptying and even death. God is never more glorious than when glimpsed in the cross. However much the world may be a theatre for the display of God's glory, revealing the majesty of the Creator to those who have eyes to see, what we see in the creation is the work of God's hands. By contrast, what we see in the humility of the cross is God's heart, the painful compassion with which the triune God has loved and redeemed the world.

It follows from all of this that to live as those who are truly in the image of God, we should have the same mind and heart as Jesus had, leaving behind selfish ambition and the urge always to seek our own interests, understanding ourselves as servants of others (Philippians 2:3–5). This is what it means to be truly godly or like God. It is also what it means to be truly and properly human, to be restored to the calling that human beings were always intended to display. That calling is now both revealed and made possible in Christ, who is like a 'second Adam', repairing and renewing the old humanity (Romans 5:12–17). The virtue of humility enables us to be set free from delusions about ourselves and to live in harmony with God, with each other and with our true identity. It helps us to be stable, fulfilled and contented in the way we live our lives. It enables us to resonate with a God whose glory consists in the willingness to give generously to an undeserving world. It promotes the well-being of the human community and increases its capacity to flourish.

(10) Friday

Christ, the bread that came down from heaven

READ JOHN 6:22–59

'I am the living bread that came down from heaven. Whoever eats of this bread will live forever; and the bread that I will give for the life of the world is my flesh' (v. 51).

From the beginning of these studies, John 1:14 has been ever close at hand: 'And the Word became flesh and lived among us, and we have seen his glory, the glory as of a father's only son.' The words are an explicit statement of the incarnation. The flow of the argument in John 1 is highly significant. The Word was in the beginning, the Word was with God and the Word was God, but then the Word became flesh. Something of the highest significance has happened. John bears witness here to the way in which the Son of God, who had been from eternity, entered into time and took to himself a specific human identity. The same idea is reiterated at various points in the Gospel and today's key text is one of those points.

In the story of Israel we encounter the time when the Israelites believed themselves to be starving in the wilderness. God provided them with a mysterious food that would appear overnight and sustained them for years until they came to the promised land (Exodus 16). It was called 'manna' (meaning 'what is it?') and was a gift from God that enabled the people to survive. In John 6, we find Jesus speaking of himself as a kind of manna: he has come down from heaven; his giving of himself upon the cross is the means by which he feeds and nurtures people so that they may live; he invites us to eat of this mysterious bread. The sharing of bread and wine in the Christian celebration of Communion illustrates what Jesus had in mind. The meal recalls Christ's sacrifice on the cross and the way in which his death and resurrection bring forgiveness and reconciliation with God. Through Christ we are restored. As, in the practice of Israel, a meal would often accompany the offering of a sacrifice, so Christians share in a meal centred on the sacrifice of Christ. As they do so, they draw life and nourishment from the self-giving Christ who is in their midst: they hold spiritual communion with him.

John 1:14 records for us both an event and an experience. The event is properly understood as the turning point of history, a pivotal moment in the human project. The eternal entered into time, the immortal into mortality, the divine into the human. It happened at a point that we can more or less accurately date. Indeed, the common calendar of the world is determined by it (although, when it was calculated, it was out by about five years). The God of Israel has always been a God who comes: God comes to his own people in their distress, and the incarnation is the supreme example of his coming. God comes to the extent that he enters into human life and experience in order to bear the load of our lost condition: he seeks and he saves what was lost (Luke

19:10). When something is lost, you have to go to the place where it is before you can find it; in the same way, in Christ, God has come to us to the fullest extent in order that he may retrieve and restore us. Christian faith is, therefore, based upon a historical reality incarnated in the person of Jesus of Nazareth. His coming was as real and as earthy as the bread and wine we share in Communion. The Creator became part of the created, but without ceasing to be the Creator.

Yet an event on its own is not enough; it is the impact of the event that counts, which is why John went on to write, '… and we have seen his glory, the glory as of a father's only son.' This was the experience of the first disciples, to see the glory of God in Jesus and to be transformed by it. In the history of Israel, the Lord God chose to live first in a tabernacle (the tent of meeting) and then in a temple. These were located in the midst of the people and were understood to be where God made his dwelling place. To worship God and draw near to him, the tribes of Israel would go up to the tent or the temple to offer their sacrifices. But now the dwelling place of God is neither in a tent nor in a building, but in a human being of flesh and blood—indeed, in Christ himself. Literally, John 1:14 could be translated as 'the Word… pitched his tent among us'; just as the glory of God was somehow contained within the tent of meeting, now it is contained in the life of Christ. He is the one in whom God may be found. Through him and his sacrifice, we can draw near to God in worship. Through him, God makes God's own self freely available to the world.

This is the experience that Christians enter into when they come to believe in Christ and, through him, enter into the truth and grace of God (John 1:14). Put in a slightly different way, it corresponds to what the apostle Paul says in 2 Corinthians 4:6: 'For it is the God who said, "Let light shine out of darkness", who has shone in our hearts to give the light of the knowledge of the glory of God in the face of Jesus Christ.' Christ is the one through whom we may encounter the glory of the God of creation. Through him we can be spiritually fed and nourished. He gives access to the knowledge and grace of God to all who receive him. He is God coming to us so that, through him, we ourselves might come to God. He is the very temple of the living God, not now confined to a building made with hands but in one who is like us, yet unique among us. This Christ is truly 'the way, and the truth, and the life' (John 14:6).

(11) Saturday

The Christ who was born of a virgin

READ LUKE 1:26–45

The angel said to her, 'The Holy Spirit will come upon you, and the power of the Most High will overshadow you; therefore the child to be born will be holy; he will be called Son of God' (v. 35).

The remarkable life of Jesus of Nazareth, as shown to us in the Gospels, is framed between two signs or miracles: the miracle of the womb and the miracle of the tomb. Jesus is singled out as being of extraordinary significance by these two 'bookends' to his life, his birth of a virgin mother and his resurrection out of death. They proclaim him to have come from God and to have God's approval in ways that no other persons have. Today's passage is one of two birth accounts (the other being in the Gospel of Matthew), which relate from different perspectives the circumstances of Jesus' birth. In Luke's version, Mary is visited by a messenger angel identified as Gabriel. Wherever angels appear in the biblical story, they are indications of the nearness and activity of God. God is at work and angels are witnesses and messengers to this effect.

The angel tells Mary that she has been singled out and that she is greatly favoured. The emphasis is upon the grace and favour that Mary has received from God rather than upon any ability of her own to impart grace, but it would be an understatement to say that Mary is being honoured by God. She is being called to bear the Son of God in her womb and to be responsible for his nurture and growth to adulthood. This was no little task. It is not surprising, therefore, that Mary has been honoured in the history of the Church's devotion with some exalted titles. She is called both the Mother of God and the God-bearer, or *Theotokos*, and it should be clear what these titles imply. In fact, they tell us more about Jesus than about Mary. They are meant to underline the fact that Christ has truly taken upon himself a full and complete human identity, being born of a woman and being born under the law (Galatians 4:4). The birth of Jesus was a normal human birth, with the exception that Christ was born of a virgin.

The virginal conception of Jesus stresses the fact that Jesus came to us as a gift from God. He was not the product of the human race, not even of the most devout and obedient Jewish parentage. It was beyond the capacity of fallen humanity to produce Jesus. He could come to us only by the inspiration and working of God, and he arose from within the human race but not as a product of it. Jesus was a work of God. In him God was converting the world back to himself and making all things new. The Word of God, through whom all things were made, who gives pattern to the universe, was now present in the midst of that creation, reorientating it to God and becoming the means of its ultimate transformation.

The birth narratives need always to be read against the

background of the story of Israel. When we read them in this way, we discover allusions that open up the meaning of Christ's coming. In Luke 1:35 the angel tells Mary, 'The Holy Spirit will come upon you', and we can see in these words a reference back to the creation narrative of Genesis 1. Here, the creative Spirit of God is said to have 'swept over the face of the waters' (Genesis 1:2), and was at work to give shape and form to the world that God was calling into being out of nothing. In a similar way, we now find the Spirit coming upon Mary to do a work of new creation, to fashion and shape in her womb one who will be holy, the Son of God. This is a new beginning for the old creation. We should not see the virginal conception as an attempt to 'explain' how it is that Christ can be both fully divine and fully human. The virginal conception was not an explanation so much as an appropriate sign of God's work through the Spirit. It was congruent with the fact that Christ came to us from God and that a new world of possibilities was opening up in him.

We should also notice that our key verse goes on to say, '... and the power of the Most High will overshadow you.' This is reminiscent of the way in which the glory of God, in the form of a cloud or a pillar of fire, overshadowed the tabernacle in which the people of Israel believed God to have made his dwelling (Exodus 40:34–38). Mary is like the tabernacle, a bodily tabernacle, with God choosing to dwell in her womb in order to be present among us.

A third reference back to the history of Israel can be found in the account of Mary's visit to her kinswoman Elizabeth, who would shortly give birth to John the Baptist. As Mary arrived in the Judean town in the hill country, Elizabeth's child 'leapt in her womb'. This was understood to be a leap for joy as John, even in the womb, recognised the one for whom he was to prepare the way (Luke 1:41, 44). Such a gynaecological wonder is not unknown to pregnant mothers, but here it was seen as a sign. It recalled the time when the ark of the covenant was returned to Jerusalem after years of exile, and King David was found 'leaping and dancing before the Lord' and doing so 'with all his might' (2 Samuel 6:12–16). As the ark was the location where God was to be found enthroned, so the throne of God's presence is now in the humble Jewish woman called Mary, and John the Baptist leaps for joy in recognition of Christ's coming. John the Baptist shows us the way and sets the tone of delight and celebration as we also recognise the coming of the 'one who was to come'. Jesus comes to us as the gracious and greatest gift of the one true God.

(12) Second Sunday

The Christ who learned obedience

READ HEBREWS 5:1–10

Although he was a Son, he learned obedience through
what he suffered; and having been made perfect, he
became the source of eternal salvation for all who
obey him (vv. 8–9).

On the whole, and despite claims to the contrary, we know quite a lot about the life, times, teaching and destiny of Jesus of Nazareth. Most of what we know is contained in the four Gospels. On the other hand, we know virtually nothing about his life between his birth and his baptism at the hands of John the Baptist. Most of Jesus' life was lived in obscurity. Nazareth itself was an obscure village with virtually no prestige at the time of Jesus. Because there was no mention of it in the Hebrew Scriptures, the town had no pedigree to boast of— although, because the name could come from the Hebrew word *netzer* (branch), it is possible that some descendants of the royal house of David settled there. The province of Galilee was regarded among establishment Jews as being somewhat suspect because it bordered the Gentile nations and was at a remove from the holy temple in Jerusalem. Being close to the main trade routes of the region, it is quite possible that Jesus would have spoken Greek as well as Aramaic and it is highly probable that, as a carpenter, he would have worked at Sepphoris, the large administrative town being built close to Nazareth. In those years, Jesus would have spent time travelling around the region, becoming acquainted with its people, its customs and its problems, and all of this experience was later to emerge in his vivid parables.

But what was Jesus really doing in those years? We might say on the basis of today's key text that he was learning obedience. The one account we do have from these years portrays Jesus as a boy of twelve, the time when Jewish boys came to adulthood, visiting the temple in Jerusalem as part of his new religious duties (Luke 2:41–52). At the end of the festival, Jesus stayed behind in the temple, questioning the teachers of the law and even venturing his own answers. Jesus was well advanced in understanding.

Reading this episode, we are troubled that Jesus seemed to be so little conscious of his parents' anxiety for him once they missed him in the travelling band of pilgrims with whom they had all come. It seems as though he was so taken up with the discussions he was having that he lost sight of them: 'Did you not know that I must be in my Father's house?' (v. 49). However, we are then told that he returned to Nazareth and was obedient to them.

Being human is about exploring and learning, and this is a universal experience. Being fully human, Jesus had to learn, as do the rest of us, and this meant learning what it meant to be obedient both to his earthly parents and his heavenly Father. Today's passage is unequivocal that Jesus, even though he was God's Son, needed to learn obedience amid the conditions of human life and nature, and to do so even though that obedience eventually cost him his life.

For many Christians, this is a difficult idea to grasp. They ask, 'Surely Jesus, as the Son of God, knew all things?' He was perfect from the beginning, was he not? But even perfection, or completeness, is something that has to be learnt. To deny that Jesus needed to learn is to deny that Jesus took a genuine part in human nature. Human brains are limited in their capacity and are programmed for the learning experience. Imagine if Jesus had studied mathematics at school. Would he have automatically got everything right, however complicated the calculations? Then there was his work as a carpenter. Would he not have had to learn how to use his tools and apply his craft, sometimes making mistakes? Perhaps Jesus was not even a particularly outstanding carpenter! If we conclude that Jesus was capable of getting things wrong on the way to getting them right, all we are saying is that in these respects he was like us: he was normal. To say anything else would be to remove him from the human realm altogether and to make him superhuman, which is not what the incarnation was about. The Word became 'flesh' (and the word has the overtone of weakness).

Hebrews 5:1–2 affirms that Jesus was chosen from among mortals, and that he was subject to weakness in the same way that we are. It is for this very reason that he is able to sympathise with people like ourselves. He is on our side. He learnt the hard way. Life was no easier for Jesus than it is for anybody, as is shown by the fact that he suffered and did so exceptionally. Yet there was one significant difference, and this is captured in Hebrews 4:15: 'But we have one who in every respect has been tested as we are, yet without sin.' Because Jesus is one with us, he is able to sympathise with us, but he was not mired in the same problem as we are: he was without sin. For this reason he is able to lift us out of our fallen condition. He was like the rescuer who comes to our aid, putting herself or himself in danger, and yet with the ability to extricate us from jeopardy. He was not overwhelmed by the sins that overwhelm us but was free from them and so was qualified to save. Having lived the obedient life as a human being and been made perfect in his love for God and for others, he has become 'the source of eternal salvation for all who obey him' (v. 9). Because he has been obedient to the Father, we now owe obedience to the Son; and, as we obey, we can know his life being transfused into our own.

Hebrews 12:2 describes Jesus as the 'pioneer and perfecter of our faith', and this is a fine way to think of him. Christ has done what no human being has done before him and so has opened up a new and living way to the Father, and a new, obedient manner of life which is pleasing to God. We should look to him and follow steadily and continually in his footsteps.

(13) Monday

The Christ who identified with sinners

READ MATTHEW 3:1–17

John would have prevented him, saying, 'I need to be baptised by you, and do you come to me?' But Jesus answered him, 'Let it be so now; for it is proper for us in this way to fulfil all righteousness' (vv. 14–15).

Jesus emerged from obscurity when he was baptised by John the Baptist in the River Jordan. This event marked the completion of the time of preparation and saw Jesus being launched into his ministry, as his calling was confirmed by the voice from heaven and the Spirit of God came upon him in fresh power. In this way a new chapter opened and Jesus came into the fulfilment of God's purpose for his life. This period lasted between one and three years, although nobody can be certain about the exact timescale. It was a time of both great popularity and intense persecution and was to result in Christ's death. These years in the life of an untrained and unordained Jewish rabbi in a downtrodden country have had an immense impact upon subsequent history, more so than the lives of any ruler or potentate, and continue to do so.

John the Baptist preached a baptism of repentance and preparation as the people of his day awaited God's great intervention in their history, which they identified as the coming of the kingdom of God. John pointed to a figure greater than himself who was to baptise not with water but with the Holy Spirit. In this sense he was a forerunner, and his baptism was a preparation for the greater blessing that was to come. Many came to him to be baptised and among their number was Jesus himself, whom John was already identifying as the 'coming one'. This threw John into a dilemma about whether or not the circumstances should be reversed, but Jesus insisted on being baptised by him in the belief that this was required of him 'to fulfil all righteousness' and to be fully obedient to God.

John's dilemma was partly to do with the fact that his baptism was about repentance, about turning back to the God of Israel. Jesus was one who was already united with God in intimate love, so why should he need to be baptised? The answer to this is surely that he did not need to be baptised; rather, he chose to be baptised as though he were a sinful person. This is what John discerned. As Jesus was the one who had humbled himself to take the form of a servant, now he humbled himself still further and, though he was without sin, took the place of sinners in identification with the lost and fallen state of Israel and the whole human race. The baptism of Jesus was an act of compassionate self-identification with those who are 'harassed and helpless, like sheep without a shepherd' (Matthew 9:36), an act in which he came 'to seek out and to save' the lost (Luke 19:10). To find those who were lost, Jesus came to the place where the lost ones were. In his baptism he freely assumed the place of the lost and alienated person. Only by identifying with them was Christ able to act on their behalf, like a priest representing the people before God.

The baptism of Jesus should be seen as more than the opening event in his ministry. It was expressive of his whole life and ministry up to that time and beyond it. It was the signature of his self-giving ministry, the distinctive characteristic of everything about him. It even anticipated his death. At a later date, he declared, 'I have a baptism with which to be baptised, and what stress I am under until it is completed!' (Luke 12:50). By this he meant the baptism of death, which he would also endure in solidarity with sinners. Just as, in baptism, a person is covered over by the waters, so Jesus would be overwhelmed by the waters of death. The baptism foreshadowed the death of Christ, therefore, in which he would give himself as 'a ransom for many' (Mark 10:45).

The Spirit came upon Jesus at his baptism to impart to him the divine strength he would need to fulfil the ministry before him. At the same time, the coming of the Spirit in this way marked the beginning of a new age, an age in which God was now acting in his Son to redeem the world and to bring in God's own kingdom to displace the kingdom of oppression and darkness. The gift of the Spirit was more than a personal gift to Jesus but was the Spirit of the new age, of which Jesus was the anointed Messiah and agent. This was another cosmic moment in which history changed gear. The age of the Spirit, and so of the fulfilment of God's purpose, had begun and nothing would ever be the same again. This was now the messianic age, when what was wrong would be put right and the crooked would be made straight—but not completely, as yet.

At the time of Jesus, there were some Jews who looked for the coming of two Messiahs. They studied the prophets and deduced from them the need for two: one would be a priestly Messiah along the lines of the suffering servant in Isaiah 53, and the second would be a triumphant Messiah, a Davidic king of great power (as described in Zechariah 14). What the New Testament offers us, however, is not two Messiahs, each of whom comes once, but one Messiah who comes twice—the first time in great humility and in identification with sinners, and the second time in great glory, 'not to deal with sin, but to save those who are eagerly waiting for him' (Hebrews 9:28). In the baptism and then the death of Jesus, we see the first coming of one who entered into our condition in order to heal it. We see that if there is to be salvation, this has to happen, that it was willed by a gracious and merciful God and that it was carried out by one whose food and drink was to do the will of the Father. Jesus was baptised in order to identify with us. When we are baptised in his name, we are identifying ourselves with him and asking to be counted in the company of those who are his followers.

(14) Tuesday

The Christ who
overcame temptation

READ LUKE 4:1–15

---

*Jesus answered him, 'It is written, "One does not live
by bread alone"' (v. 4).*

Strangely, the first thing that happened to Jesus after his
baptism and endowment with the Spirit was not that he
embarked upon his mission but that he was led by the Spirit
into the wilderness to be tested. This is more than a way of
saying that a spiritual high point was followed by a period of
spiritual struggle, although that is a common human experience. Part of Jesus' mission was to overcome the power of evil
in the world. He would soon be setting people free from evil
influences (see Luke 4:31–33). It needed to be known from
the beginning that Jesus himself had overcome temptation
and that he was crystal clear in his inner being about his
identity and calling. At the heart of all that Jesus did and said
was deep personal integrity. We might say of Jesus not that
he practised what he preached but that he preached what

he practised. His teaching and spiritual authority came out of the depth and quality of his inner spiritual life. He was entirely successful in overcoming temptation, so much so that the passage tells us both that he was led by the Spirit into the wilderness and that he returned to Galilee in 'the power of the Spirit' (v. 14). The experience of temptation served only to strengthen his spiritual life.

Although Jesus may well have experienced a prolonged period of spiritual wrestling in the wilderness, we are also entitled to infer from this passage that the temptations recorded were recurring ones. At the end of this episode, we are told, the devil departed 'until an opportune time' (v. 13), which suggests that further testing would follow. Indeed, there is only one way in which we can know about these temptations and that is if Jesus had opened his heart to his disciples about them.

In Mark's much shorter version of the events, we are told that Jesus was 'with the wild beasts' (Mark 1:13). This phrase is immediately reminiscent of the account of Adam and Eve in the garden of Eden. They too were with the wild beasts, but whereas those parents of the human race yielded to temptation, as have all their descendants ever since, Jesus swam against the tide and succeeded where we have failed. He emerged from the wilderness hungry but unscathed. As in the story of Adam and Eve, a great deal was at stake, because the primary question in all of the temptations was, 'In what direction shall I live my life?' For Adam and Eve, the answer was to disregard God and collapse into self-centredness and self-exaltation, but Jesus made the decision to live by the word of God, to worship God alone. He refused to treat God as though God exists for the benefit of humanity, acknowledging rather that we are here for his glory. The direction of Jesus' life was to live as one who is completely available for the service of God and the divine purpose.

Jesus' temptations were high-level and subtle ones, relating not to small matters of momentary concern but to Jesus' very identity. In two cases the words occur, 'If you are the Son of God...' (vv. 3, 9). Jesus had just come from his baptism, holding in his mind the words, 'You are my Son, the Beloved' (Luke 3:22), and it was at this point that he was being tested. What did it mean to live as the Son of God? How must he faithfully live out this identity and vocation? Was there an easier way of doing what God wanted, one that involved the spectacular use of divine power while avoiding the suffering of which he was already becoming conscious? This was the test that Jesus must have wrestled with throughout his life as he sought to work out how he might fulfil God's will.

As Adam and Eve were tempted by the serpent in the garden, so here Jesus is tempted in the desert, and the tempter is still a deceiver. In life there are many alternative ways that seem superficially attractive and enticing but actually lead nowhere. The devil claimed that all the kingdoms of the world and their glory had been given over to him, and that he could dispense them to whomever he willed, but this was a lie. These things actually belonged to the one who was being tempted, and he was their rightful Lord. Now, just as he did not count equality with God something to be exploited or grasped but took the form of a slave (see Philippians 2:6–7), so he set about the patient and difficult task of winning back the kingdoms of the world, not through the use of worldly and domineering power but by patient, self-sacrificial suffering. The temptations Jesus faced here were essentially the same as those he experienced in the garden of Gethsemane, which received the same response: 'Abba, Father, for you all things are possible; remove this cup from me; yet, not what I want, but what you want' (Mark 14:36).

It would be a strange person who never wondered why God does not sort the world out swiftly and effectively by the exercise of omnipotent power. Why does God not simply speak a word, as he did at the creation, and put the world to rights? Apparently, the God in whom Christians believe has chosen an infinitely more difficult way. God's preferred pathway is to renew the world from within, not to adjust it remotely from without. All of this is part of the foolishness of God that is wiser than human wisdom, and the weakness of God that is stronger than human strength (1 Corinthians 1:25). Jesus overcame temptation and showed that he was not a prisoner to the fallen human condition: he was a free person, free for God and God's service. He lived over again the story of the first human beings and changed the outcome. This was a sign of hope that human beings can overcome temptation and that they can follow in his footsteps with his help. It is essential for followers of Jesus, as for Jesus himself, to be true to our identity, to live as those who have become children of God and of the light, to be clear about the direction in which we are called to live our lives—for God and God's glory alone. 'For once you were darkness, but now in the Lord you are light. Live as children of light' (Ephesians 5:8).

(15) Wednesday

Christ and the law of love

READ MATTHEW 22:15–40

---

*He said to him, '"You shall love the Lord your God
with all your heart, and with all your soul, and
with all your mind." This is the greatest and first
commandment. And a second is like it: "You shall
love your neighbour as yourself." On these two
commandments hang all the law and the prophets'*
(vv. 37–40).

Jesus was not a 'Christian'. He was a devout and practising
Jewish believer, and it is impossible to understand him apart
from this identity. 'Christians' come into the picture later as
those who believe and trust in Christ (Acts 11:26). We are
not to think of Jesus, therefore, as someone who was careless
about the Jewish law and its expectations. In fact, he taught
that he had come not to abolish the law and the prophets
but to fulfil them, and that their righteous demands would
never in themselves be superseded (Matthew 5:17–19). God
would always require holy living.

Jesus fulfilled the demands of the law by living in complete obedience to them and in this sense he became, in the words of the apostle Paul, 'the end' of the law (Romans 10:4). By this Paul seems to mean that Christ embodied in his own life the purpose and intention of the Jewish law and, because this was the case, followers of Jesus now look to his example as the expression of what the obedient life looks like. Although they may still learn from the law, for Christians Jesus' own life has become the new law, the dynamic expression of what God wills, which surpasses, completes and carries forward everything that has gone before. Jesus did not see himself relaxing the demands of the law but extending them: the righteousness of his followers was to exceed that of the scribes and Pharisees (Matthew 5:20). He increased the law's demands by stressing that more than outward conformity was required: righteousness was about inward holiness, about the transformation of the heart.

In verses 34–40 of our passage today, we see Jesus caught up in a debate about which was the greatest commandment. An expert in the law of Moses asked for his opinion, although not with a completely pure motive. In the Hebrew Scriptures, there are 613 commandments and, although each one is important, most people would agree that some are more important than others. This might lead to the conclusion that one commandment must be the most important of all. Jesus was quite clear in his response. The first and greatest commandment was to 'love the Lord your God with all your heart, and with all your soul, and with all your mind'. Combined with a second commandment to love one's neighbour (taken from Leviticus 19:18), this was the key to understanding the whole of the law and prophets. As it happened, Jesus was not saying anything new: others had said similar things before. The words Jesus cited as the first commandment were taken from Deuteronomy 6:4–5 and were recited by every devout Jew twice a day, morning and evening. The expert in the law already had the answer to his question. Jesus was simply making it unavoidable.

The unavoidable truth about love is that it has to come from the heart. The kind of love enjoined by the scriptures and by Jesus himself is complete and undivided love for God— love with a whole heart. When we see it like this, we may understand how Jesus could be the 'end' of the law, in that he embodied whole-hearted love for God and for neighbour: he was the incarnation of what it means to love. The law— all those 613 commandments—may help us to understand what love looks like in concrete detail and specific acts, but it is love that enables us to complete them. This is how the law and the prophets all depend upon the first and greatest commandment.

Jesus was, in fact, fulfilling an ancient expectation voiced by the prophets of Israel. Speaking from God, Ezekiel had said, 'A new heart I will give you, and a new spirit I will put within you; and I will remove from your body the heart of stone and give you a heart of flesh. I will put my spirit within you, and make you follow my statutes and be careful to observe my ordinances' (Ezekiel 36:26–27). Jeremiah had said likewise, 'I will give them a heart to know that I am the Lord; and they shall be my people and I will be their God, for they shall return to me with their whole heart' (Jeremiah 24:7).

The state of a person's heart was of utmost significance to Jesus, since it is out of the heart that the mouth speaks (Matthew 12:34) and it is from the heart that evil intentions come (Mark 7:21). Although the law was good and righteous, it was not enough on its own to create good people. It could indicate what the good life might look like but could not deliver it without a change of heart. Jesus called people to experience an inner conversion and a new beginning, to 'change and become like children' in order to enter the kingdom of God (Matthew 18:3). They needed to take the opportunity that God was giving them, through his own presence and preaching, to repent (Mark 1:15).

As we saw at the start of today's reflection, Jesus was not a Christian in the way that his subsequent followers are: everything about him was faithfully Jewish. He was circumcised according to the tradition; he kept the law, worshipped in the temple and observed the Sabbath, and did so with a keen eye for the inner meaning and significance of his actions. He was calling people not to a new religion but to a rediscovery of what the people of Israel had borne witness to from the beginning. The effect of this was to expand the reach of the God of Israel far beyond the boundaries of the Jewish people, while not for one moment excluding them from their own inheritance. Jesus' interpretation of the law made love for God and neighbour central to its nature and fulfilment. It majored on the heart's being transformed with love for God and becoming the wellspring of a quality of life that cannot be achieved in any other way.

(16) Thursday

Christ the prophet

READ MARK 6:1–13

---

*'Prophets are not without honour, except in their
hometown, and among their own kin, and in their
own house' (v. 4).*

The passage we are reading today suggests that Jesus saw
himself as a prophet and that he identified with the prophetic
tradition of the people of Israel, among whom such people
were not always welcome. As we encounter Jesus in these
verses, we notice that he is now well embarked on his public
ministry. He has begun to make an impact upon the region
as a teacher, a healer and an exorcist. Wherever he went,
extraordinary events happened: evil influences were removed
and people excluded from the community by longstanding
disabilities were restored to health and fellowship by Jesus'
word and touch. Jesus was a powerful and beneficial presence.
Yet, as is sometimes the case, those who had most difficulty
recognising him in this newly prominent role were residents
of his own home town in Nazareth. They could hardly
believe that the carpenter with whom they were so familiar

could cut this kind of figure. There is even the suggestion that members of Jesus' own family, his own 'house' (v. 4), were having difficulty with these new developments. Jesus pondered wistfully the fact that prophets do not receive much honour among their own, and in this we catch a glimpse of his consciousness of being a prophet.

Prophets speak the word of God to the people. They are impelled by the Spirit of God to speak words that come from beyond their own imagination but are mediated through it. They reveal urgency in the way they speak because they feel the word of the Lord in their bones. Their words are powerful, and this is part of their undoing. They do not simply predict what is about to come; they make it happen by the words they utter. Because their words are powerful, they are seen as bringing about the events of which they speak, and, if those events are catastrophic, the prophets are reckoned as the cause of the catastrophe—'troublers of Israel' (1 Kings 18:17). As a young man, Jeremiah was appointed 'over nations and over kingdoms, to pluck up and to pull down, to destroy and to overthrow, to build and to plant' (Jeremiah 1:9–10). No wonder that people could be wary of those who believed themselves to be prophets. In particular, the prophetic word was feared by the powerful, the wealthy and the established, since it often exposed their abuses of power and their lack of faithfulness to the covenant God had made with Israel. This was a tradition in which Jesus clearly stood.

Yet there were significant differences between Jesus and other prophets. This was not only because he was a prophet of the good news of the kingdom rather than of coming judgment (though he struck that note, too). The typical prophetic formula contained the saying, 'Thus says the Lord', and prophets saw themselves as being mouthpieces for God, rather in the way that Aaron was for Moses (Exodus 4:10–

17). Jesus never used this formula but instead was prepared to declare, 'You have heard that it was said… but I say to you' (Matthew 5:21–22, 27–28, 31–32, 38–39). In other words, rather than ascribing his words to the Lord for whom he was simply a mouthpiece, he presumed himself able to interpret the present meaning of God's law and to speak with authority. He knew the mind of God. He referred to his own authority and this displayed the fact that, although he was a prophet, he was much more. He was, in a more weighty sense, the presence of the God of Israel in their very midst.

This pushes us in the direction of saying also that it was not only Jesus' words that were prophetic but also his actions. John the Baptist was invited to draw his own conclusions about Jesus from the works that he did: 'Go and tell John what you hear and see: the blind receive their sight, the lame walk, the lepers are cleansed, the deaf hear, the dead are raised, and the poor have good news brought to them. And blessed is anyone who takes no offence at me' (Matthew 11:4–6). But even this is not enough: it was not only the words and the deeds that formed Jesus' prophetic ministry but his very self. We return here to the idea that Jesus was the Word of God, spelt out in terms of an incarnate human existence (John 1:14). His very person and being were communicating the truth about God, so that when he was stirred with righteous indignation or moved with great compassion, when he wept over Jerusalem (Luke 13:34) or spoke words of forgiveness to a dying criminal (23:43), when he prayed for those who were crucifying him or restored a failing disciple (23:34; John 21:15–22), he was speaking to us, in his actions, about the God from whom he had come.

Prophets should be heeded. Their words are meant to bring us to our senses and to bring us into life. If it can be said of John the Baptist that he was a prophet 'and more than a prophet' (Luke 7:26), how much more should we believe this of Jesus? We are to live 'by every word that comes from the mouth of God' (Matthew 4:4). The Christian life is a discipline of constant and concentrated listening to Christ. For those who are serious about such a way of living, there is no way of bypassing the prophetic witness of Jesus to the Christ-like God. Although we are to honour every part of the scriptures and seek to hear the word of God through them, nowhere are we more likely to hear that word than through the Gospels, which bear their immediate testimony to Jesus' life, death and resurrection. They occupy a particularly honoured place in the Christian scriptures. The Hebrew writings that built up to this singular life are to be read as preparation for his coming, and the Greek scriptures that we call the New Testament can be seen as recollection of that life through which God has spoken most clearly and eloquently to this world. The life of Jesus is the core and centre of the Bible. It acts as the key by which we may understand the wider drama of Israel and of the early Church and the word of God that is spoken through them.

(17) Friday

Christ the priest

READ LUKE 10:1–24

---

*'All things have been handed over to me by my Father;
and no one knows who the Son is except the Father,
or who the Father is except the Son and anyone to
whom the Son chooses to reveal him' (v. 22).*

We commonly refer to Jesus of Nazareth as 'Jesus Christ' and, in so doing, are making large claims. The word 'Christ' is not so much a name as a title referring to the fact that Jesus is regarded by his followers as the Messiah or 'Anointed One', which is what the Greek word 'Christ' means. At his baptism, Jesus was 'anointed' by the Spirit and so initiated by God into the office of the Messiah, which he then went on to fulfil.

In the Gospels, the confession of Jesus as Messiah occurs more often on the lips of his followers than of Jesus himself. In a place called Caesarea Philippi, Jesus asked his disciples what people on the streets were saying about him. They responded by giving him the results of their polling data: 'Some say John the Baptist, but others Elijah, and still others Jeremiah or one of the prophets.' Jesus then went on to ask what must reckon as the most important and directly personal question of all time: 'But who do you say that I am?' Simon Peter's response was, 'You are the Messiah, the Son of the Living God.' Jesus then declared that this had come to Peter by revelation from the Father (Matthew 16:13–17). The recognition that Jesus was the Messiah was a decisive moment, a pivot on which the rest of the story would now turn.

In the history of Israel, three kinds of people were 'anointed', either literally with oil in a specific ceremony or metaphorically by the Spirit. An example of the latter is the prophet upon whom the Spirit descends: 'The spirit of the Lord God is upon me, because the Lord has anointed me; he has sent me to bring good news to the oppressed.' These words from Isaiah 61:1 were taken up by Jesus with reference to himself when he opened his ministry with his sermon in Nazareth (Luke 4:18). Besides prophets, priests and kings were more literally anointed with oil as a sign that God had chosen them. The rite for ordaining the high priest, Aaron, is described in Leviticus 8, and both Saul and David serve as examples of kings being anointed by the prophet Samuel (1 Samuel 10:1; 16:13). The rite specifically indicated that these people were chosen by God for their office and responsibility and equipped by his wisdom and Spirit. In the case of Jesus the Messiah, the calling he received should be seen as being to a threefold responsibility as prophet, priest and king. This 'threefold office' has long been seen as a comprehensive and helpful way of describing the work of Christ. Yesterday we looked at the dimension of prophet and tomorrow we shall be concerned with that of king, so today we focus on the priestly dimension.

There is much to be said under this heading, and we shall return to it later. The idea that Christ is our great high priest is a major theme of the book of Hebrews. It is impossible to address this issue without recognising that Christ's death is to be understood as an act of sacrifice and that he is both the priest and the sacrificial offering, in that he gave not an external object but his very self for us (Hebrews 9:11–14). The idea of priesthood is also broader than this, however. The priest acted as a mediator between God and the people. He (in the practice of Israel, priests were male) represented God to the people and the people to God, and could act both for God and for the people. The priest would both intercede before God for the people and bless them in the name of the Lord. Through the sacrificial offerings, the faults of the people were covered over and removed, so that God could continue to be among them and they could continue to draw near without fear. The idea of constant mediation was central.

It is in this context that we can take note of the saying of Jesus that is today's key verse. Here Jesus claimed that the only one who knows him truly and fully is the Father, and the same is true the other way round: only the Son truly knows the Father. This reveals to us Jesus' own awareness of his unique relationship to the God of Israel: there is no one like him in this regard. This is the ultimate priesthood, of which all other kinds of priesthood are a mere reflection. Of course, this claim is either woefully mistaken or gloriously true. As it happens, Christians believe it to be true. Jesus uttered these words at this time because he celebrated the fact, as revealed in the earlier part of this chapter, that his work of making the Father known, of mediating the Father, was actually bearing fruit.

Jesus claimed that he knew the Father and was able to make the Father known. He had the freedom and the authority to make the Father known to whomever he chose to reveal him. His persistent use of the term 'Father' here suggests to us that Christ is able to draw others into intimacy of relationship with God, the same quality of relationship that Jesus himself knew and expressed when he called the Father 'Abba' (Mark 14:36). The apostle Paul speaks of that intimacy as being a gift from the Spirit, who enables us to make this worshipping confession (Romans 8:15–17). What was particularly distinctive here was not the claim to mediate God in some way: this is a common claim of religious teachers. Rather, it was about knowing the God of creation and Israel in the intimate way that we know a father who is close and who cares. Jesus' band of disciples were among the number to whom Christ made this deep reality known, and were the firstfruits of many others who were to follow. But we can set no limit to how widely, how often and to how many Christ can reveal the Father. 'For there is one God; there is also one mediator between God and humankind, Christ Jesus, himself human, who gave himself a ransom for all' (1 Timothy 2:5–6).

(18) Saturday

Christ as king

READ MATTHEW 27:11–37

Over his head they put the charge against him, which read, 'This is Jesus, the King of the Jews' (v. 37).

The Messiah Jesus was anointed by God as prophet, priest and king. We might imagine that he resembled a prophet and a priest more than he ever could a king. Jesus was, by anybody's standards, an unusual kind of king, the kind that overturns all our preconceptions of what a king is meant to be. The profound irony of a crucified rabbi being hailed a king is captured in the cynical notice that hung above Jesus as he was dying: 'This is Jesus, the King of the Jews.' John's Gospel underlines the point by telling us that this notice was written in Latin, Greek and Hebrew (John 19:20), so that no one could fail to understand.

We have noted how, at Caesarea Philippi, a major turning point was reached when Peter understood and confessed Jesus as the Messiah, the Son of the Living God. Strangely, however, Jesus was reticent about this new recognition of his status and immediately commanded his disciples not to tell anyone (Matthew 16:20). Scholars of the Gospels have often drawn attention to what they have called 'the messianic secret'. Although the Gospel writers readily identified Jesus as the Messiah, Jesus appeared hesitant to do so himself. The rest of Matthew 16 suggests that before Jesus could be publicly and openly proclaimed as Messiah, he needed to redefine what the term meant and what people assumed from it. Jesus went on to tell his disciples that he was constrained to go to Jerusalem, where he would suffer and be killed. This was not what people were expecting. The very same Peter who had just been commended for seeing the truth clearly then took Jesus to task and declared that this should not be allowed to happen. In so doing, he revealed that his own understanding of the Messiah was faulty. The people of Israel were expecting a warrior to come who would set them free from Roman oppression, but this is not the kind of messiah that Jesus was. He had not come to take life, not even the life of a single Roman soldier, but to give his life as a ransom for many (Mark 10:45). Here we are speaking of serious redefinition.

Jesus' life from this point would involve going up to Jerusalem, not to kill but to be killed. He invited his disciples to take up their cross and follow him, to take part in the same kind of non-violent sacrificial action that he himself engaged in at great personal cost (Matthew 16:26). It was in this way that the kingdom of God would come. To acknowledge Jesus as our king involves following him in this regard and 'becoming like him in his death' (Philippians 3:10). Jesus was certainly a different kind of king, but he claims our loyalty and we should submit to his reign. We find in the Gospels that Jesus' undoubted authority was exercised to do people good, to heal them of their diseases and set them free from their afflicting spirits (Mark 1:32–34). Whereas earthly kings commonly used their power and authority to take from their people and amass wealth and prestige for themselves (1 Samuel 8:10–18), Jesus used his authority to set people free and restore them to wholeness, leaving himself with nothing. He was a servant king.

Nobody can claim that following Jesus is easy. Following him to the cross is the hardest thing of all. Yet we have not seriously come to grips with Christian discipleship until we have wrestled with the 'hard texts' that contain Jesus' most demanding teachings. We are tempted to explain them away. When we read that we should turn the other cheek or go the extra mile (Matthew 5:38–42), we typically seek to discover all the ways in which such commands do not apply. Bishop John Saxbee has recounted how the Danish philosopher Kierkegaard once observed that had Jesus said, 'Follow me and you will have comfort, wealth and possessions beyond the dreams of avarice', we would say to ourselves, 'I understand full well what that means. Yes, I'll follow, and where do I collect the money?' But Jesus actually said, 'Take up your cross and follow me.' Suddenly, we need commentaries and professors of biblical studies to show us how Jesus did not mean, or possibly did not even say, 'Take up your cross'—and if he did, he did not mean his words to apply to us! Yet Jesus overturns our values and assumptions and calls us not to be conformed to this world (Romans 12:2). Jesus' kingdom is an upside-down kingdom in which things are done differently, according to a higher logic.

In his preaching, Jesus proclaimed the gospel of the kingdom of God, which had come near and which his hearers could enter by repenting of their sins and believing his message (Mark 1:15). The kingdom of God was that future horizon to which they looked forward, and through which they imagined a time when all things in heaven and earth would be subject to God's gracious reign. Jesus taught, however, that this future was already present. It was possible to experience it now and live according to its demands and expectations. In his preaching, it had arrived, and he was the king of this kingdom, with the royal right to call others to follow him and accept his authority. But this requires a major re-evaluation of what we count important in the present. Humanity's relentless obsessions with money, sex and power will not change the world and make it a better place, but will only drive it down more deeply into the mire. Jesus redeemed the world by self-giving sacrifice, the willingness to suffer and to die for the sake of others. His style of kingship was one that absorbed evil and put a stop to the vicious cycle of recrimination. His kingdom was about showing forgiveness and having mercy on others, about love for God and for neighbour. It is still this kind of living that will redeem the world and turn things around for good. Living in the kingdom of God means living under the sovereign reign of a very different kind of king who, although disregarded in the short term, will in the long term be universally vindicated as Lord of all.

(19) Third Sunday

Christ the teacher

READ MATTHEW 5:1–26

---

*When Jesus saw the crowds, he went up the
mountain; and after he sat down, his disciples came
to him. Then he began to speak, and taught them
(vv. 1–2).*

These words begin the acclaimed 'Sermon on the Mount',
which contains some of Jesus' most famous teaching. Here
he assumed the classic position of a Jewish rabbinic teacher,
since, when a rabbi instructed his followers, it was customary
for him to be seated while the disciples remained standing.
Around him were his disciples (a word that means 'learners'),
and they in particular were the subjects whom Jesus was
instructing with his own brand of wisdom. Yet around them
we are to imagine a greater crowd who, at the end of the
sermon, are said to have been 'astounded at his teaching, for he
taught them as one having authority, and not as their scribes'
(7:28–29). The reference here is to the way in which typical
Jewish scholars would base their words on other rabbinic
scholars regarded as authorities. By contrast, Jesus spoke from

82

himself as a unique interpreter of the sacred writings and their contemporary significance. Jesus had a depth of insight and personal conviction that lent him a striking and compelling degree of authority.

A picture is now beginning to build of the kind of person Jesus was. He had a deep intimacy with the God of Israel, whom he addressed, unusually for the time, as 'Father'. He saw himself as having a commission from the Father to preach about repentance and the kingdom of God. He accompanied his preaching with acts of healing and exorcism, which were signs of the new power that was now present in Israel, liberating people from spiritual distress and laying the foundations of a movement of renewal within Israel. Yet these developments were not happening with the permission of the Jewish religious authorities based in the temple in Jerusalem but at a distance from them, a distance which meant that Jesus represented a threat to the present power holders.

It was not that Jesus was aiming to found a new religion. Rather, he backed up what he was doing with a well-thought-out alternative form of Judaism, which, while respectful of all the traditions of Israel and rooted in the Hebrew Scriptures, was at the same time reinterpreting them in non-violent messianic terms. Scholars point out how, in Matthew's Gospel, Jesus is actually portrayed as a new Moses. The book divides itself into five sections that correspond to the five 'Books of Moses'. Later in that Gospel, when Jesus is 'transfigured', the disciples with him see Moses and Elijah appear to him: these two figures symbolise the Law and the Prophets, of which Jesus was the fulfilment (17:3). The Sermon on the Mount was reminiscent of Moses going up Mount Sinai to receive the Law from God, and so we might see Jesus here giving a new law and a new revelation.

Although Jesus ministered widely to the crowd, he also

took time to instruct his close disciples patiently and more privately. In his teaching he employed a whole variety of communication methods, including prophetic acts (like the entry into Jerusalem, which echoed Zechariah 9:9) and parables that intrigued and, at times, puzzled those who heard them. By universal consent, Jesus was a master of the art of the parable. Contrary to popular belief, he did not always tell these stories to clarify issues, as though they were illustrations of the truth. Instead he used them to obscure his teaching, so that only those who entered imaginatively into them and thought about them with an open mind and a degree of faith would really grasp them: 'The reason I speak to them in parables is that "seeing they do not perceive, and hearing they do not listen, nor do they understand"' (Matthew 13:13).

In addition, though, Jesus taught in plain language, sometimes adopting a poetic metre (such as in Matthew 5:3–11) in order to make his words memorable. The Sermon on the Mount is usually regarded not as a single sermon, delivered just as it is on one occasion. There would be a great deal to digest if it were. Rather, it should be seen as a collection of sermons delivered at different times but gathered together in one literary collection by the Gospel writer, to pass on to the next generation of Christians. Perhaps we might see it as a compilation of Jesus' greatest words and sayings.

The fact that, 2000 years on, there are numerous disciples around Jesus, listening carefully to what he had to say, is sufficient evidence of the fact that he was a great teacher. He appeals to people of diverse cultures and instincts across the world, who wonder at his wisdom and authority. The circle of those who are listening to him includes more than just Christians. A Hindu teacher like Gandhi could appreciate and be guided by Jesus' approach to non-violent protest, for example. Increasing numbers of Jewish believers now recognise Jesus as one of their own, who imparted a compelling interpretation of Torah (the Jewish Law), which stands the test today—especially noting, in his command to love our enemies, a new departure in Jewish thought. Secular hearers may rubbish the Church but find it much harder to dismiss Jesus. Rather incredibly, some even claim him as one of their party. But such contemporaries can benefit from his teaching only because it has been preserved and passed on by the Christian Church. Sometimes the first Christians did not fully understand what Jesus meant, but they passed his teaching on anyway, just because it was he who had said it.

Although the Christian faith is much more than intellectual enlightenment, it is certainly not less than that. Hearing, seeing and understanding the truth that is in Jesus is part of what God gives to us in him. Jesus is our teacher and guide, our sage and our interpreter of the ways of God. He is the way and the truth as well as the life. We cannot get away with cosily quoting Jesus' sayings or retelling his stories, imagining that they are easy to understand. They are not. First of all, we have to give them our careful attention, seek to indwell and inhabit them until they become second nature to us, and wrestle with and ponder the sayings we do not understand or that seem downright impossible to us. Then we might grow in inner wisdom and understanding of the gracious ways of the mysterious God.

(20) Monday

Christic the controversialist

READ LUKE 21:1–28

---

*'For I will give you words and wisdom that none
of your opponents will be able to withstand or
contradict' (v. 15).*

Jesus had different ways of communicating his message.
We have seen how these included parables and more direct
ways of teaching, and how he preached to the crowds and
instructed his disciples privately. He was also a very able
controversialist, used to arguing his point and defending
himself against the rhetorical devices of others. Examples of
this can be found in Matthew 22:15–33, where Jesus gets the
better first of some Pharisees and then of the Sadducees in
arguments about paying the tribute tax to Caesar and about
the resurrection.

Public controversy is also a form of communication. It
means that accepted ideas can be challenged and new ways of
thinking put on the table. We also gather from these debates
that Jesus was a contested figure; it was by no means the case
that his teaching was regarded as acceptable. He was seen as

a potential threat to the well-being of Israel, so much so that there were plots against him. These would, of course, come to fulfilment in his trial and arrest by the Jewish authorities, and then in his crucifixion by the Romans. It was convenient for them to have Jesus put out of the way. This was not the universal attitude of the religious teachers but it had enough support to prove successful.

Jesus was controversial because he had a different inter-pretation of the direction that Israel should take. He could see that the likely outcome both of the Jewish establishment's collaboration with the Romans and of the violent opposition to Rome of more militant Jewish groups, like the Zealots, would be Jerusalem's destruction. Today's passage represents a strand of Jesus' teaching as he looked forward. Apocalyptic passages such as this are often read as though they refer to the end of the world, but the nature of apocalyptic is that it draws upon the past and anticipates the future while also referring to the present. It tends to use dramatic cosmic language such as 'There will be signs in the sun, the moon, and the stars' (v. 25) to refer not to the dissolution of the natural order as such but to 'earth-shattering' events in history that evoke fear and distress. The future then becomes telescoped, with forthcoming events seen against the background of the ultimate future, in order to bring out the fact that they are part of the judgment of God.

All the evidence suggests that Jesus had a strong intuition about what would happen to Jerusalem, foreseeing it sur-rounded by Roman armies (v. 20). In fact, he stood from time to time on the Mount of Olives, with its panoramic views of the city, at exactly the same spot where, some 40 years later, the Roman legions would make their camp before destroying the city in revenge for the Jewish rebellion against Caesar's rule. All of this Jesus had foreseen, and had called Israel to another and better way, but his call was too controversial to be heard. Some of his most poignant words were uttered on the Mount of Olives at a place (so it is supposed) now occupied by a small chapel in the shape of a teardrop and known as Dominus Flevit, 'the Lord wept': 'Jerusalem, Jerusalem, the city that kills the prophets and stones those who are sent to it! How often have I desired to gather your children together as a hen gathers her brood under her wings, and you were not willing!' (Matthew 23:37). Jesus was controversial not because he proclaimed a way of rage and violence but because he summoned those who would listen to him to love their enemies, including the Romans (5:43–48). For any of us, this is a hard word to hear, most especially when suffering oppression and injustice. But nowhere do we hear the distinctive voice of Jesus more clearly than at this point, and nowhere do we, like Jerusalem, find it more difficult to respond to the challenge.

To love our enemies does not mean that we should not argue our case with forcefulness and conviction, as Jesus did. The ability to debate and argue remains a part of Christian communication now, as it was in Jesus' own ministry. This is why he reassured his disciples that even when the pressure was on them, they should take the opportunity to testify, and they need not be afraid for he would give them 'words and a wisdom that none of your opponents will be able to withstand or contradict'. That they would have opponents was a certainty; that they would be spoken against and contradicted was beyond doubt. But it was equally certain that they would be given the gift of sure speech, in order to testify well to the Christ in whom they believed.

Christian testimony will always be controversial, since, like Jesus, Christians owe their first loyalty to a kingdom that is not 'of this world' (John 18:36). This does not mean that Christ's kingdom is concerned only with some future or heavenly realm, but rather that it does not operate according to the preoccupation with power and domination that characterises the kingdoms of this world. Followers of Jesus play the game of life in a different way: they are concerned with giving rather than gain, with sacrifice rather than aggression, with setting people free rather than making them captive. This will always be beyond the comprehension of the powerful and mighty, yet it is the way that will lead to life. For as long as the human race, like Jerusalem, refuses to follow it, it dooms itself to tragedy and self-destruction.

In this kind of world, the Christian Church needs skilled communicators who have learnt from Christ the words and wisdom needed to testify to his kingdom in the present. In an age in which we have never had so much information at our fingertips, we should grasp the fact that information is not the same as wisdom. Wisdom is knowing how to interpret information and how to apply it courageously and accurately to particular circumstances, even when it goes against the grain of popular or established opinion.

(21) Tuesday

The Christ who was afflicted

READ MATTHEW 26:26–46

Again he went away for the second time and prayed,
'My Father, if this cannot pass unless I drink it, your
will be done' (v. 42).

Isaiah 53:3 says of the suffering servant, 'He was despised
and rejected by others; a man of suffering and acquainted
with infirmity.' It is not surprising that the early Christians
were to find in this verse, and actually in this whole chapter,
a prophetic reference to Christ. After the times of popularity
and acclaim, the underlying notes of opposition that had
been present from the beginning of Jesus' ministry were to
become dominant, issuing in his rejection and finally in his
arrest, trial and death. In today's reading we encounter Jesus
'grieved and agitated' (v. 37), 'deeply grieved, even to death'
(v. 38). It is as though a huge weight of sorrow descended
upon Jesus as he neared the end of his life and mission. If
purpose of life is the pursuit of happiness, then Jesus
arly failed to achieve it. His death was the opposite of
v of us would wish for ourselves: he was rejected by

his opponents, forsaken by his friends, tested and tried to his limits, and died the cruel death of crucifixion.

Jesus was not the only person to have suffered in these ways but, given the kind of life he lived and the person he was, there is an added poignancy to his case. He drank the cup of suffering to the dregs and, in so doing, made his identification with fallen and suffering humanity complete. Jesus has been there; he has tasted death and done so in a way that was undeserved and unwarranted. His suffering was unfair and unjust, but the fact that he endured it qualifies him to speak and act for us. It lends him moral authority.

Today's reflection begins to confront us with the dreadful outcome of Jesus' life. It is an unlikely theme to have at the centre of a world religion, but then the Christian faith is inherently unlikely. If we were constructing a religion, we would certainly have neither the imagination nor the guts to put a suffering Messiah at the heart of it. Yet through the years, the faith of Israel had been developing to the point where it could give birth to just this idea. The God of creation, whose very presence spelt death to any person who entered it without certain carefully prescribed precautions, had come to be seen increasingly as a God who was with his own people even in their suffering. To the idea that the Lord was holy and righteous, there came to be added the notion that he sympathised with those whom he called his own: 'In all their affliction he was afflicted, and the angel of his presence saved them... he lifted them up and carried them all the days of old' (Isaiah 63:9, RSV). When the Israelites were sent into exile in Babylon and experienced the devastation of loss, they came to build even this experience into their understanding of God. They glimpsed the possibility that even through this experience, God was with them, redeeming his people—a faith that they articulated in the songs of the suffering servant, who gave his life for the sake of the people (see Isaiah 53). Through these slow but steady insights, the possibility that their God might be a God who entered into their suffering in the most personal way possible began to emerge. Against all the odds, they saw that the entry of God into their sorrow could bring healing to them.

As we have seen, the idea that the Messiah could be one who suffers and dies was a thought that the first disciples grasped only with extreme difficulty. Only after the resurrection were they able truly to come to terms with it. Knowing that they would desert him, Jesus mused on the text from the Hebrew Scriptures, 'I will strike the shepherd, and the sheep of the flock will be scattered' (v. 31, citing Zechariah 13:7). We find it hard to believe that God himself was striking Jesus, as a first reading seems to suggest. As we think more deeply about it, however, we might see in this verse Jesus' own awareness that the suffering he was about to endure was not outside the purposes of God, that even these events could be folded back by the infinitely creative God into God's purpose to bring salvation. In Gethsemane, Jesus prayed that the cup of suffering might pass from him, but he also recognised that there was a necessity to his suffering that was according to the will of God. Only Christ identifying himself with human beings to the most extreme limits was enough to redeem their condition.

Some years ago, Mel Gibson's film *The Passion of the Christ* depicted the afflictions of the Saviour in the most prolonged and graphic form. By contrast, the Gospels are reticent in the extreme about the sufferings of Christ. We are told enough for us to know what happened, but we are not encouraged by the text of scripture to wallow in the details. The depiction of a suffering Christ is remarkably restrained when compared with some traditions of religious art. Yet we are told enough for us to realise that a sanitised, idealised Christ is not what we should have in mind. Jesus truly suffered, and his end was the final destination of a journey on which he had been engaged since he set his face to go up to Jerusalem (Luke 9:51–53).

As the writer to the Hebrews tells us, 'Therefore he had to become like his brothers and sisters in every respect, so that he might be a merciful and faithful high priest in the service of God, to make atonement for the sins of the people. Because he himself was tested by what he suffered, he is able to help those who are being tested' (Hebrews 2:17–18). No Christian should believe that they are immune from suffering. If Jesus suffered, then we are likely to know suffering too, but God is not absent from us in our suffering. Though our pain might threaten to drive thoughts of God away, the truth is that God is with us and does not forsake us.

The Christ who died in our place

READ MATTHEW 27:15–26

Pilate said to them, 'Then what should I do with Jesus who is called the Messiah?' All of them said, 'Let him be crucified!' Then he asked, 'Why, what evil has he done?' But they shouted all the more, 'Let him be crucified!' (vv. 22–23).

It is a core Christian belief that Christ died to save us and that human beings are altogether dependent on what he has done for them on the cross. Being mired in their fallen and sinful inability consistently to do what is right, they need someone to act as a Saviour, to lift them up. Recognising this is the first step in being a Christian. Having previously emphasised the way in which the Son of God has come from God to identify with us in the extremity of our plight, we may now see that Christ saves us by participating in our condition in such a way that he can be said to 'bear' it, and in bearing it he remedies it (1 Peter 2:24). This might be described as a doctrine of 'salvation by participation'. Christ comes to us, becomes one of us and acts with us and for us. The whole life of Jesus is part of this work of salvation, but in dying on the cross he goes to the final limit, revealing the extent of God's redeeming love. We might say that God goes further than ever before to restore us to himself, and that there is no further that God could go and nothing greater that could be done. In the familiar text, 'For God so loved the world that he gave his only Son' (John 3:16), the word 'so' has a dual meaning: it is in this self-giving way that God has loved us, and it is to this great extent that such love has been shown.

The death of Christ is certainly a 'mystery'. By this we do not mean that it is impossible to understand but rather that it is so dense with meaning, it means so many things and has so many dimensions, that it is not a simple task to capture these meanings in words. Standard accounts of the atonement employ varieties of images, metaphors and theories to bring to expression what God has done in the cross. The great majority of them are drawn from suggestions in the New Testament itself, and none of them is sufficient on its own to give an account of the atonement. Because the Gospels are primarily narratives, we can look to the way in which the crucifixion is described and related there to discover their interpretation of the cross. Today's reading contains the account of Barabbas being set free and Jesus taking his place upon the cross. This is a powerful illustration of God's purpose in his Son and of the saving work of the cross.

The situation described is one of mob rule. The mob is rarely a pretty sight and hardly ever acts reasonably or kindly. Human failings are intensified when they come together in an unthinking and aggressive crowd. The suggestion here is that they have been whipped up by the leaders of the religious establishment, most of whom would be aristocratic members of the Sadducee party (v. 20). Jesus Barabbas was a 'notorious prisoner' who is described elsewhere as an insurrectionist and a murderer (Luke 23:19). He was a guilty and corrupt man, a violent and dangerous criminal, and for his crimes he was due to die, cruelly but not unjustly. This would be the outcome of the way he had lived his life. Two other criminals, or 'bandits' (Matthew 27:38), would die with Jesus, and the third cross, on which Jesus was impaled, would have been the one intended for Barabbas.

By contrast with Barabbas, Jesus did not deserve to die. He was recognisably innocent (vv. 19, 23) but, by a combination of conspiracy on the part of the powerful and compliance on the part of the mob, Jesus was chosen to be executed in place of Barabbas—the innocent for the guilty. Jesus Christ took the place of Jesus Barabbas. Every time we repeat the Apostles' Creed, we remind ourselves that Jesus was 'crucified under Pontius Pilate'. All that we know about Pilate suggests that he was cruel and ruthless. He was concerned, in the trial of Jesus, not with bringing justice but with extricating himself from an awkward situation that he probably did not fully understand. He washed his hands of the situation and then 'released Barabbas for them; and after flogging Jesus, he handed him over to be crucified' (v. 26).

This was the fulfilment of Jesus' own words: 'For the Son of Man came not to be served but to serve, and to give his life a ransom for many' (Mark 10:45). A ransom is a price paid in order to set someone free. The analogy derives from the slave market, where slaves might be redeemed by the payment of the appropriate price. The death of Jesus was the price paid to set free the human race, and the first, obvious person to benefit was Barabbas. Like Barabbas, by the direction of our lives and by our choices and actions, we have brought down upon ourselves a fate that we deserve, one that estranges us from God and leads to spiritual and personal death. Yet Christ has made our death his own death and has taken our place in such a way as to absorb and remove our fate. He has been 'made lower than the angels... so that by the grace of God he might taste death for everyone' (Hebrews 2:9). Barabbas was the first person who might have chosen to say, 'Christ died for me.' In him we can see a picture of what all those are able to say, who trust in Christ as the Saviour who died for them.

Nobody knows what happened to Barabbas. It is probable that he returned to his life of crime. Books have been written and films made in which endings to his life have been supplied. Some have him being haunted by the image of Jesus on the cross until he finally submits to him and embraces Jesus' death as a sacrifice for himself. We do not know. But we can know how our own lives might end, and what it might mean for us to define ourselves in the light of a Saviour who has taken our place and made himself a ransom that sets us free.

(23) Thursday

The Christ who was abandoned

READ MATTHEW 27:27–56

---

*And about three o'clock Jesus cried with a loud voice,
'Eli, Eli, lema sabachthani?' that is, 'My God, my
God, why have you forsaken me?' (v. 46).*

For the Christian, the point at which Jesus of Nazareth
uttered these words in his identification with lost humanity
is the most poignant of all. The words are known as the 'cry
of dereliction' and are drawn from Psalm 22:1, in which
the psalmist records the feeling of being utterly disregarded
by God—a sense of what we might call the acute absence
of God. There are many resonances in this psalm with the
drama of Jesus' life. Some commentators rush to point out
how, by the end of the psalm, the psalmist has recovered
confidence and hope, but we should not move too swiftly in
that direction in case we overlook the depth of Jesus' grief and
sorrow. The way Matthew tells it, the cry was accompanied
by a period of darkness lasting three hours, as the light of the
sun was blotted out. To all appearances, the light that shone
in the darkness had been overcome (John 1:5). Nature was

participating in the terrible moments of Christ's experience of God-forsakenness. It was an earth-shattering event: in recognition of it, the earth shook and the rocks were split as though creation itself were in crisis with its Lord, bearing witness to the awful nature of the events. The Messiah who dared to call God by the intimate name of 'Abba, Father', and of whom the voice from heaven had declared, 'This is my Son, the Beloved, with whom I am well pleased' (Matthew 3:17), now experienced what it was to be bereft of God. If this account were not so familiar to us, it would be almost unthinkable.

It is hard to believe that the Father had actually forsaken the Son, yet it is beyond doubt that this was the Son's experience. He journeyed so deeply into human alienation from God, into the far country away from God, that the Son shared in what it was like to be finally lost, to have passed over the edge and lost God fully. This should not be understood as Jesus' loss of trust in God but as his enduring, in our place, the ultimate fate of those who forsake God. How long this experience lasted is not known to us. Was it for a moment in time only or for an extended period?

We read in Isaiah, 'For a brief moment I abandoned you, but with great compassion I will gather you. In overflowing wrath for a moment I hid my face from you, but with everlasting love I will have compassion on you, says the Lord, your Redeemer' (Isaiah 54:7–8). These words were spoken to indicate how Israel's exile from their homeland was God's judgment on their persistent lack of faithfulness. It is as though Jesus was experiencing exile. Israel was to be thrust from God's presence because of her sin:

And now, because you have done all these things, says the Lord, and when I spoke to you persistently, you did not listen, and when

I called you, you did not answer, therefore I will do to the house that is called by my name, in which you trust, and to the place that I gave to you and to your ancestors, just what I did to Shiloh. And I will cast you out of my sight, just as I cast out all your kinsfolk, all the offspring of Ephraim (Jeremiah 7:13–15).

Although cast in an active mode, this passage describes how God allowed a foreign empire to overcome Judah and bear her children off into exile. In the same way, the Father allowed his Son to be crucified at the hands of the Romans, but this was no accident. It was 'according to the definite plan and foreknowledge of God' (Acts 2:23) that these things happened. It was all woven into the divine purpose to redeem the world by Christ's participation in the depths of its lost condition. In no sense should the crucifixion be seen as the Father's displeasure with the Son but as the Father and Son together enduring the consequences of human sin in order to redeem humankind.

We should not wish to evade the plain biblical testimony that rebellion and disobedience against God bring us into judgment. Yet this is a judgment of our own deserving, something that we call down upon ourselves as a consequence of our own actions. In the garden of Eden, Adam and Eve had been told that they might freely eat of any tree in the garden, with one exception: if they did eat of that one tree, they would surely die (Genesis 3:3). So it proved, although the death they died was one of spiritual estrangement from their Creator long before it became physical death. The judgment of God should be seen primarily as God's determination to give us over to the consequences of our own choices. This is how it is portrayed in Romans, where Paul explains three times that, since human beings failed to honour God and turned to lesser things, God 'gave them up' (Romans 1:24, 26, 28) to endure what they had brought upon themselves. This 'giving up' is the active judgment of God, the expression of the divine wrath against sin. Its immediate result is estrangement from God and therefore from our true natures. Its ultimate result, if left without a remedy, is eternal death in place of eternal life, the loss of our destiny in the friendship and eternal love of God. It is this death that Jesus tasted for us on the cross, and that was the reason for the cry of dereliction.

If judgment is the act of God in giving us up to the consequences of our actions, we should notice that precisely the same language is used of the cross. Romans 8:32 indicates that 'he who did not withhold his own Son, but gave him up for all of us, will he not with him also give us everything else?' Christ 'gave himself for us that he might redeem us from all iniquity' (Titus 2:14). Christ has been given up, and has willingly given himself up, to take upon himself the consequences of human sin and to bear them in his body on the tree, in order that those for whom he has died might be redeemed from their self-inflicted fate. This is how the one God—Father, Son and Spirit—has so loved the world.

(24) Friday

Christ our sacrifice

READ HEBREWS 10:1–25

And it is by God's will that we have been sanctified
through the offering of the body of Jesus Christ
once for all (v. 10).

We have noticed how Matthew's Gospel communicates
theology to us in narrative form: the story he tells contains
details that hint at its meaning. Nowhere is this clearer than
in Matthew 27:51, where we are told that at the moment
in which Jesus breathed his last, 'the curtain of the temple
was torn in two, from top to bottom.' The curtain of the
temple separated the Most Holy Place in the building from
the other courts that surrounded it. Here, the Jews believed,
God made his dwelling place and reigned invisibly enthroned
above the ark of the covenant. So holy was this place that it
could only be entered once a year, on the Day of Atonement,
and only by one person—the high priest, who had to take all
due precautions before doing so. These precautions included
offering sacrifice for himself before he could make sacrifice for
the sins of all the people (Leviticus 16). The whole structure

of the temple, and the pattern of sacrifice that accompanied it, were meant to communicate a clear message: God was holy and therefore remained at a distance from his own people. He could be approached only with the greatest care, and only through sacrifices by which the sins of the people were confessed and removed. In this way, the people could remain assured of God's presence with them and his favour towards them.

In the light of this background, which had shaped and formed the thinking of the Jewish people for many centuries, the image of the tearing of the curtain was of immense significance. The way was opened up into God's presence. The separation of the people from their God could now be overcome. There was now a 'new and living way that he opened for us through the curtain (that is, through his flesh)' so that we may 'approach with a true heart in full assurance of faith' (vv. 20–22). This was a sacrifice that did not need to be repeated time and time again but happened 'once for all' (v. 10).

Properly understood, sacrifices can be offered because they are provided by God himself (Genesis 22:8). In the Hebrew Scriptures, they are many, varied and at times complicated. They can be understood as offerings of thanksgiving to God but also as the means of being cleansed from sin. The underlying logic was that when we sully and pollute our own lives, those lives need to be made clean again. The blood of the sacrificed animal was believed to contain life, so when the blood was shed, it was like the release of life to renew the one who had been polluted. When the one who offered the sacrifice laid hands upon the animal, he or she was identifying with it, such that its shed blood was effective on his or her behalf. Of course, even in the Hebrew Scriptures, this ritual was seen primarily as symbolic. The sacrifices that really counted were in the person's own heart: 'For you have no delight in sacrifice; if I were to give a burnt-offering, you would not be pleased. The sacrifice acceptable to God is a broken spirit; a broken and contrite heart, O God, you will not despise' (Psalm 51:16–17).

The book of Hebrews makes it clear that the sacrificial system of the temple and the priesthood were temporary forms of instruction, in preparation for the day when Christ's once-for-all sacrifice would be offered. Animal sacrifices could cleanse from ceremonial and ritual infringements but could not address the real sin of the human heart (10:11). The self-offering of Christ, however, was one that reached to the heart of the human problem. As Jesus bore the sins of many and poured out his life, he was acknowledging the sinful and fallen condition of human beings and God's righteous judgment upon them. At the same time, by living a life of full obedience to God, even as far as submitting to death, he was offering to God the thing that humans have failed to give and that God may rightly require of us—a completely devoted and holy life. In doing this, Jesus was the one who stood in the breach for humanity, who 'made intercession for the transgressors' (Isaiah 53:12). He therefore became the grounds for our abundant and confident access to God as restored sinners.

On a number of occasions, the New Testament describes Christ's death as an 'atoning sacrifice' for our sins (Romans 3:25; 1 John 2:2; 4:10). The Greek words used on these occasions have been variously translated, but one of them properly means 'a place of atonement', referring to the lid of the ark of the covenant, which was sprinkled with blood on the Day of Atonement. The self-offering and sacrifice of Christ on the cross may therefore be seen as the place where atonement takes place, the place to which we may come to be cleansed from our sins and restored to the presence of the holy God. It is here that God has met with us in space and time, yet that place of atonement is not confined to past history. When it is proclaimed in preaching, or recalled in baptism with its imagery of dying and rising, or celebrated in Communion, the sacrifice of thanksgiving that finds meaning in bread and wine, the place of atonement becomes a reality in the here and now. Because the offering was once for all, it need never be repeated: it holds good for all time. But its impact and life-transforming power are renewed and repeated every time we revisit the 'place of atonement' in imagination and in faith.

It is, of course, a benefit of believing in Christ as the once-for-all sacrifice that we need never return to animal sacrifice in our worship practice. Although, when we read about them in the Hebrew Scriptures, they have power to illuminate the sacrifice of Christ for us, such sacrifices have been fulfilled, surpassed and rendered unnecessary by the work of Christ. What are now needed are lives that are living and grateful sacrifices, 'holy and acceptable to God' in response to God's love for us (Romans 12:1).

(25) Saturday

Christ the reconciler

READ 2 CORINTHIANS 5:11–21

*In Christ God was reconciling the world to himself,
not counting their trespasses against them, and
entrusting the message of reconciliation to us (v. 19).*

To confess Jesus Christ as the Saviour upon whom we depend for salvation, and without whom we are without hope, requires that we have some understanding of what we need to be saved from. The people of Israel began to understand that the Lord was their Saviour once they had experienced the mighty deliverance at the Red Sea: 'Do not be afraid, stand firm, and see the deliverance that the Lord will accomplish for you today' (Exodus 14:13). Impending annihilation or return to captivity focused their minds on their need for salvation, and once they had been delivered, they certainly knew it.

To interpret the cross, Christians have pressed many images into service and, in different ages, one or other of these images may have experienced a particular prominence. In the early centuries, the Church gave particular emphasis to the idea that the death of Christ was a ransom payment that sets us free. In the Middle Ages, the stress fell more on the cross as an offering to God that satisfied divine honour. After the Reformation, more attention was given to the notion that the cross was the enduring of a penalty on our behalf. The images at these different times were drawn from the ransoming of captives in war or of slaves at the market, the need to pay due honour to the feudal ruler, and the kind of justice that is delivered in the court room. Much Protestant thought has been strong on legal images to do with guilt, punishment and acquittal (or 'justification'). Previously in this book, the preferred idea has been that of divine participation in our human condition, and this too has a long pedigree in Christian thought, summed up in the fourth-century words of Gregory of Nazianzus: 'What has not been assumed has not been healed.' God heals the world (using at this point a therapeutic image) by bearing and absorbing its sickness as though it were his own.

One image we can explore further is the idea of reconciliation, mentioned in our key verse for today: 'In Christ God was reconciling the world to himself.' Reconciliation is a clear theme in this passage from 2 Corinthians, and it is an image that relates to the family. The parable of the prodigal son speaks directly to this condition (Luke 15:11–32). We are like children who have spurned their father, wished him dead and squandered their inheritance on useless things. In the process, we have brought ourselves into crisis and damaged ourselves. We have also become estranged from those who are our brothers and sisters. But there is a way out. We can come to ourselves and return to the Father. Far from rejecting us, he will welcome us and celebrate our homecoming. More than this, the Father does not wait for us to come to our senses but comes looking for us and enables us to turn back in repentance. When we are ready to return, we find that there is already a way made for us to do so, for the good news is not primarily about our seeking and finding God but about God coming to us in order to seek us. In one sense, when people talk about 'ways to God' and whether there is only one way or many ways, the Christian should turn the conversation round by 360 degrees. The gospel is about God's coming to us and to all the world before it is about our coming to God.

Surprisingly, the notion that 'relationship is everything' is a relative newcomer to the intellectual scene. Only with the development of the disciplines of psychology and sociology have we begun to grasp, with fuller insight, that it is impossible to be healthily human without being in relationship. Relationships are the very means by which our humanity takes shape: we are what our relationships allow us to be. Loving relationship is the most valuable asset that any person can have. Those who understand the biblical approach to humanity should find this idea entirely convincing. The God we worship is a relational God—Father, Son and Spirit—and we have been created in this image, as male and female, as relational persons. To be estranged, then, or to fall out of relationship, damages our essential identity and means that we lose ourselves.

Genesis 3, the narrative in the Bible that describes human nature most penetratingly, is, at root, all about the loss of relationship. There is a loss of communion with God, which precipitates human beings into disruption. They become alienated from themselves in that they are ashamed of being naked, as God made them (Genesis 3:10). They are alienated from each other in that they begin to blame each other and fight (vv. 12, 16). They are alienated from the creation that they were called to steward and tend (vv. 17–19). Suddenly Eden, which means 'bliss', has become a bad dream. The peace of creation has been vandalised. Human beings have fallen from their true destiny, which was to live in harmony with God, themselves, each other and creation. We are children who are estranged from the Father who has loved us with everlasting love.

Once we understand this, we may see how fundamental is the theme of reconciliation. In Christ, God was about the business of restoring relationship with himself. The aim of the cross was to provide a way by which those who are lost and estranged might find a way back, enabling them to face the truth about themselves (because the cross reveals that truth) and at the same time to know that their past lives have been judged and replaced with the obedient self-offering of Christ on their behalf. Yet this is only the case because the one God who is Father, Son and Spirit has acted in grace to heal, restore and accept us, and has made all the running in doing so. At the cross we can learn to accept that we are accepted, even though we continue to find ourselves unacceptable.

(26) Fourth Sunday

The risen Christ

READ I CORINTHIANS 15:1–19

For I handed on to you as of first importance what I in turn had received: that Christ died for our sins in accordance with the scriptures, and that he was buried, and that he was raised on the third day in accordance with the scriptures (vv. 3–4).

Jesus of Nazareth died and that should have been the end of it. Typically he would have passed into history as just another messianic pretender who got it spectacularly wrong, but this did not happen.

A fascinating aspect of recent research has been the way that Jewish scholars have begun to rediscover Jesus. There may be continuing disagreement between Christians and Jews as to whether Jesus was the Messiah, but that has not stopped Jewish scholars from hearing Jesus with new ears, not as the name in which they have sometimes been shamefully persecuted but as an authentically Jewish voice. A number of details emerge from this research, which help to set Jesus in context. Among these is the place

Galilee had in first-century Israel as a free-thinking and at times troublesome province, and its tendency to produce charismatic itinerant rabbis and sages, some of whom were credited with mighty acts and with exorcisms. Like Jesus, they had their disciples and devotees. Jesus, apparently, was one among many—yet every one but Jesus has been lost to history, until their memory has been more recently recovered from obscure rabbinic sources. Jesus must have been different.

Why is it that Jesus has been remembered and others all but forgotten? Indeed, Jesus has been more than re-membered: he has become the religious figure to whom over two billion people of the earth's current population offer allegiance, at least nominally. There are many reasons why Jesus might have been remembered, which touch upon the quantity, quality and content of his teaching. But the greatest reason must be the belief held by his disciples that, after he had been crucified and was most certainly dead and buried, he was raised out of death into the life of the resurrection. They might just have been mistaken, but not many intelligent commentators are prepared to argue that the resurrection was all a big hoax (although there have always been a desperate and unconvincing few). The first Christians were sincere about what they believed, and this is widely acknowledged. What they believed was that he had been raised.

Despite the claims of some Christian apologists, it is unlikely that the resurrection of Christ will ever be recognised as a 'proven' fact of history. How do you prove an event that goes beyond all our recognised canons of interpretation? Christians will firmly believe in the resurrection and will argue that it is the most coherent explanation of the evidence that is before us. They will do this, in part, because they are aware of the risen Christ in their own experience, prayer and worship. It is, however, virtually impossible to prove any event in ancient history beyond doubt, and historical discussion will always leave a certain amount of choice as to whether to believe in the resurrection or not. Yet what must count as beyond historical contestation is that the first disciples of Christ firmly believed that Jesus was raised from the dead. Without this belief, it is almost impossible to see how the Christian movement could have got off the ground once its leader had been put to death. Something exceptional motivated them. There is a world of difference between a group of disconsolate and disappointed people commemorating a dead hero, and a missionary movement boldly proclaiming that death has been defeated. Without the resurrection we would have had the former, but what we actually have is the latter. For their conviction, these early witnesses were prepared to become martyrs.

The account given by Paul in 1 Corinthians 15 is among the very earliest witnesses that we have to the resurrection. The letters of Paul predate the writing of the Gospel accounts (although not the material contained in those Gospels) and this one was probably penned no more than 20 years after the resurrection itself. However, in summarising the matter, Paul is referring back to what he himself received (v. 3), presumably when he was converted to Christ on the road to Damascus. This happened in the first decade after the Christian movement began, and so we are being drawn back into very early traditions that were probably passed on to new converts when they were baptised. The nature of these words as an early tradition is also suggested by the rhythmic form of the text, as though it has been designed to be memorised, and by the use of the name Cephas for Peter (v. 5). This was Peter's Aramaic name and suggests that the tradition Paul is passing on goes all the way back to the first, Aramaic-speaking community of disciples in Jerusalem. So we have a chain of testimony that reaches from the first disciples, who were witnesses of the risen Lord, down to ourselves, who have received and believed this tradition. In between are the millions who have lived and died in this faith.

'If Christ has not been raised, your faith is futile and you are still in your sins,' says Paul (v. 17). Everything hangs on the resurrection: whether it happened or not determines whether Christianity is 'true'. We might debate whether, even if it were not true, it would be still be worth believing in Christianity in some way—as an idealistic aspiration to a better world, for instance. Some would argue that the Christian 'metaphor' would nonetheless exercise a dignifying and humanising effect on the world. It would still be 'the greatest story ever told', able to illuminate our brief, if futile, lives. This may be so; but the apostle Paul endured 'danger from rivers, danger from bandits, danger from my own people, danger from Gentiles, danger in the city, danger in the wilderness, danger at sea, danger from false brothers and sisters' and countless privations, all for the sake of what he believed was most certainly true (see 2 Corinthians 11:23–29). It is hard to imagine how he could have felt anything but short-changed by life were not Christ indeed risen.

(27) Monday

The Christ of the appearances

READ LUKE 24

While they were talking about this, Jesus himself
stood among them and said to them,
'Peace be with you' (v. 36).

On the third day after Jesus had been crucified, the first day of the week, the women who had taken note of where Jesus was buried went again to the tomb to complete the preparation of his body for burial, a procedure that had been interrupted by the onset of the sabbath. They found the tomb empty and were perplexed. At this time they had certain visionary experiences in which they were told that Jesus was risen from the dead. When they reported these experiences to the other disciples, they were not immediately believed. As Peter was then to discover, however, the tomb was indeed empty (v. 12). Yet, at this point, these early witnesses did not deduce from the empty tomb that Jesus was alive. Instead they looked for more obvious explanations, of which the first was that someone had removed the body (John 20:13). The tomb had to be empty if Jesus was indeed risen, but on its own that fact was not enough to persuade the disciples that Jesus was alive. Something else had to convince them.

The disciples believed that Christ was risen from the dead because they experienced a series of appearances in which Christ was made known to them. Truth to tell, the accounts of these appearances can seem somewhat confusing to today's readers. The order and location in which they happened is not totally clear, although the Gospel accounts are quite specific that Jesus appeared first of all to Mary Magdalene (John 20:11–18). This in itself is held by many to be unusual, because in first-century Judaism women were not regarded as reliable witnesses. Perhaps this is why Paul lists Peter, not Mary, as the first recipient of an appearance (1 Corinthians 15:5). There are also elements of the narratives that seem to be heightened for dramatic effect, such as the earthquakes, the rolling back of the stone and the frightening appearance of the angels (Matthew 28:2–4). But even if we choose to take these details with a pinch of salt, at the heart of these accounts there is solid and multiple testimony to the fact that Christ appeared. This begins to become persuasive, and the empty tomb becomes supporting evidence for a conviction primarily derived from elsewhere—living encounters with the risen Christ.

Today's passage contains several of Christ's post-resurrection appearances. The first listed here is to two disciples walking to Emmaus. Jesus fell in with them unrecognised and engaged them in conversation about their hopes and confusions concerning the Messiah. Rumour had begun to reach them about visionary experiences that some of the women disciples had had, and about the empty tomb (vv. 22–23). These rumours posed massive questions for them. As Jesus broke bread at the meal he shared with them, they finally recognised who he was (v. 31). On returning to Jerusalem and the other disciples, they found that Christ had already appeared to Simon Peter (v. 34). While they were talking, Jesus himself appeared to the whole group; he did so in bodily form, though in some ways different from his pre-resurrection form, since he could appear and disappear.

Luke ends his Gospel with an account of the ascension. He went on to begin the second volume of his work, the book of Acts, with the ascension of Jesus after 40 days of appearances (Acts 1:1–3), so it seems that in his Gospel he was truncating the narrative for literary reasons. The ascension was a natural way to end the Gospel, even though there were other resurrection appearances that could have been described and were probably available to his readers in other writings (Luke 1:1–4). In Luke's glimpses into the resurrection experiences, we begin to see what it was that changed the disciples from broken and disillusioned people into the bold and confident witnesses they shortly became.

In the light of Luke's account, Paul's summary of the resurrection appearances, which occupied us yesterday, takes on new depth. He says nothing about the empty tomb, although it is implied in the fact that Jesus was buried (1 Corinthians 15:4), but moves directly to the appearances. Jesus appeared to Cephas (Peter), then to the Twelve (which might mean the core group of disciples in the upper room), then to a large group of followers (which Paul numbers at 500), then to James the brother of Jesus, who, we have good reason to believe, was not at first a follower but became one as a result of this meeting (Mark 3:20–21, 31–35). Then he appeared to 'all the apostles', which might have been a larger group than the Twelve, and finally to Paul himself. Paul ranked his own encounter with Christ as being of the same order as the previous appearances. His dramatic conversion from chief persecutor to dynamic apostle was itself a startling testimony to the intense and creative events at the origins of the Christian faith.

The resurrection of Jesus has always been contested. For some, dead people do not return to life and that is the end of the matter. Resurrection does not figure in their worldview because it would subvert that worldview. For Jesus to have been raised requires us to believe that there is more to this world than just the material reality we see around us, the closed universe of cause and effect. For others, what is around them in the material universe is not all there is: there is this and there is more; there is a reality beyond this reality, which finds manifestation in and through it. Far from ruling the resurrection out because it does not fit our preconceived assumptions, it confirms the belief that this is not a closed universe but an open one, capable of responding to God's creative words and doing so, sometimes, in a startling manner. There will always be an element of choice in how open we are prepared to be to new ideas—the revelation in the present of a realm of higher possibilities. For those who are open in this way, the resurrection is a sign of God's ability to do more than we imagine or think. For those who are not open, it is a challenge to think again.

☙

(28) Tuesday

The Christ who abolished death

READ 1 CORINTHIANS 15:12–34

For since death came through a human being, the
resurrection of the dead has also come through a
human being; for as all die in Adam, so all will be
made alive in Christ (vv. 21–22).

The distinction belongs to Jesus Christ of having abolished death: 'This grace was given to us in Christ Jesus before the ages began, but it has now been revealed through the appearing of our Saviour Jesus Christ, who abolished death and brought life and immortality to light through the gospel' (2 Timothy 1:9b–10). He has set free 'those who all their lives were held in slavery by the fear of death' (Hebrews 2:15). People can have the wrong idea about the resurrection. It is not that Jesus came back from the dead like Lazarus did, with his body resuscitated, some day to die again (John 11:1–27). Rather, Christ has definitively and finally destroyed the power of death. He has now been raised beyond the mortal sphere into the life of God. Not only does death not now have any hold on him; it need not have a hold on anybody: 'Christ, being raised from the dead, will never die again; death no longer has dominion over him' (Romans 6:9).

The Hebrew Scriptures reveal to us some mysterious 'near-death' experiences undergone by faithful servants of God. The first to be mentioned is Enoch, of whom it was written, 'Enoch walked with God; then he was no more, because God took him' (Genesis 5:24). What this means in precise terms is beyond anyone's knowledge, but the suggestion is that he was spared the experience of dying and was assumed into God's presence in an extraordinary way. Similarly, the prophet Elijah was also spared the experience of death and instead ascended into heaven in a whirlwind, travelling in or accompanied by a chariot and horses of fire (2 Kings 2:9–12). This was a dramatic way to go and must be seen, once more, as an exceptional act of God. Jewish thinking had room, therefore, for outstanding servants of God to end their days in non-standard ways, even being spared death. But Jesus was not spared death: instead, he 'tasted' death for everyone by enduring a particularly brutal end (Hebrews 2:9). Whatever dying and death may be all about, therefore, Jesus underwent them.

Indeed, there are large questions here. What is death? Is it simply the cessation of life, or is there a journey on which death takes us, so that there is some kind of destiny after death, a life either in God or apart from God? The parable of the rich man and Lazarus certainly seems to suggest that death is more than extinction and that there is something with which to reckon beyond death (Luke 16:19–31). Even if we agree that the details of this parable belong to the story Jesus tells (actually a well-known story in Jesus' day, which he adapted for his purpose) and are not to be taken literally, it is certainly part of his purpose to confront his hearers with the reality of death and subsequent judgment. Beyond death, for both the rich man and Lazarus there was a reversal of roles. Whereas Enoch and Elijah are portrayed as circuiting this journey of death, Jesus underwent it. He was spared nothing, but passed into death before being retrieved from it into the life of God and, in consequence, was dramatically raised from the dead. He endured all of this in order that he might take death on and subdue it.

Today's passage portrays death as an enemy that will one day finally be abolished by Christ (v. 26). His journey into death was God's way of subverting and overthrowing death, breaking its power and revealing that it had been overcome, pending the day when it will be removed altogether. The fact that death was not avoided but was undergone by Christ is a revelation of the way in which God normally works, not enabling us to avoid the difficulties and tragedies of life, but strengthening us to live through them and triumph beyond them. This does not mean that we do not die; rather, that for those for whom Jesus is the resurrection and the life, 'even though they die, [they] will live, and everyone who lives and believes in me will never die' (John 11:25–26). We die, therefore, but the 'sting of death' has been taken away (1 Corinthians 15:56), and this makes the thought of death easier to bear. Rather than being seen as the final enemy, death can be seen as the end of life on this earth and the gateway into greater life.

Christians understand that, through his death and resurrection, Christ has blazed a trail and that we may follow him. His resurrection was the firstfruits of a harvest that will come (1 Corinthians 15:20–23), he was the pioneer of our salvation, and he will bring many sons and daughters to glory (Hebrews 2:10). The resurrection of Jesus acts as the signpost for the future, showing how the mortal will one day be clothed with the immortal and death will be swallowed up in victory

(1 Corinthians 15:43–44, 54). The apostle Paul understood this acutely when he proclaimed, 'If the Spirit of him who raised Jesus from the dead dwells in you, he who raised Christ from the dead will give life to your mortal bodies also through his Spirit that dwells in you' (Romans 8:11). This is the hope that draws Christians on and encourages them to imagine an otherwise unimaginable future, to believe that everything that leads to and makes for death in the present has already been overcome through Christ's resurrection and that the final victory will follow.

It is well known that those of traditional Jewish faith differ from Christians over whether Jesus is the Messiah. Jewish thinking rules this out, since when the Messiah comes he will put all things right; because the world still moves on its way to death, Jesus cannot have been the Messiah who restores all things. For Christians, he is, because when he came he conquered death and opened the way to resurrection. For them, the final abolition of death is just a matter of time and of quiet patience.

(29) *Wednesday*

Jesus Christ the victor

READ COLOSSIANS 2:6–19

He disarmed the rulers and authorities and made a public example of them, triumphing over them in it (v. 15).

Martin Luther described the death of Christ as a victory over five tyrants—the tyrants of sin, wrath, death, hell and the devil. If this is accurate, then the victory is a comprehensive one. Everything that holds human beings in thrall, all that distorts and destroys their lives, has been overcome by God in Christ. Christ has taken them on, endured and absorbed the worst they can do and triumphed nonetheless. This is the price paid for the salvation of the world. However, to describe an ignominious death by crucifixion as a victory is, to say the least, counter-intuitive.

Some may wish to say that the cross was an apparent defeat, but the resurrection was God's act of victory that reversed the defeat. This would be a natural thought. It would be more subtle to say, however, that the cross itself was the victory and the resurrection was the revelation and proclamation of that victory. The cross was a victory in that here was a human being, representing us all, who, unlike every other human being who has ever lived, refused to walk the way of disobedience and self-exaltation, even though that refusal cost him his life. Jesus' victory consisted, therefore, in the refusal to submit to the tyrants that sought to dominate and intimidate him.

In this way, the cross can be seen as the continuation of what we encounter in the temptation narrative, when Jesus unswervingly refused the alternative pathways offered to him, and also in his baptism, in which he identified with sinners in a way that would eventually lead to his being overwhelmed by the 'baptism' of death. Furthermore, Jesus was not put to death by forces that compelled him. At any point he could have called down 'more than twelve legions of angels' (Matthew 26:53) and he would have been delivered at once. Jesus had 'set his face to go to Jerusalem', to the grim fate that awaited him there (Luke 9:51). He went there out of obedience, to fulfil the saving purpose of the Father willingly and freely. When he prayed in the garden of Gethsemane at the foot of the Mount of Olives, that the cup might pass from him, he could within ten minutes have walked up the mountain and into the dark Judean desert, never to be seen again. Yet he chose to do the Father's will and drink the cup of suffering to the full (Luke 22:39–46).

For many people, the presence of so much suffering in the central events of the Christian story is deeply offensive. In some religions, the association of God with such degrading events as crucifixion and death verges on blasphemy. How can these things be related to the majesty, excellence and beauty of the incomparable God? For other, more secular people, it is as though Christians seek to glorify suffering and verge on a form of theological sado-masochism. Why else would they have all those crucifixes and other tortured images in their church buildings? Worse still, some say, the cross and its accompanying events might even be justification for inflicting pain and abuse on others in the mistaken belief that it is 'good for them' and 'redemptive'. Such thoughts fall far, far short of the reality of which we read in the Gospel narratives. God in Christ endured suffering in order to overcome it. He went into the danger zone in order to decontaminate it. This was done freely and willingly, out of love, not for the sake of making others suffer but as God's way of identifying with a suffering world and its victims in love. It was the means by which the whole world might finally be delivered from its present groaning and bondage to decay (Romans 8:21).

In taking the way to the cross, Jesus defied the dominant powers of his day. He refused to be overcome by the abusive religious power of the Jewish establishment based in the temple; he refused to capitulate to the political powers of Rome by absenting himself from the scene; he refused to yield to the baying cries of the mob that was whipped up against him. He lived free from all these powers in order that he might be devoted to doing the Father's will alone. The cross was not the sign that these powers had defeated him, but precisely the opposite—that they could not beat him into submission, even though the outcome was that he would lose his life. This was extreme heroism by anybody's standards, and his death was most certainly a martyr's death. Yet none of these admirable ways of describing it is enough. Christ's sacrifice on the cross is not to be explained apart from the love of God of which it is an expression. Neither can it be understood unless we grasp the mysterious wisdom of God, according to which evil is overcome 'not by might, nor by power, but by my spirit, says the Lord of hosts' (Zechariah 4:6). God's way was the way of endurance and absorption, taking hatred, defiance and hostility into himself and overcoming it by the greater power of love. The cross is the pre-eminent sign and revelation of God's way of redeeming the world, overcoming by means of freely embraced sacrificial suffering.

According to today's key verse, Christ disarmed and disempowered the 'rulers and authorities' by the cross and resurrection, showing that, when ranged against the love and goodness of God, their power was fleeting. This was done publicly through the resurrection, which spelt out that the death of Christ was not a defeat but a victory. It was the ultimate act of civil disobedience, the proclamation that worldly powers will not finally win the day but have been overcome. God's loving purpose may be temporarily resisted. God's servants might be individually silenced. Not every battle in the cause of righteousness will be successful, but God will have the last word. Death will be swallowed up in victory and sorrow and sighing will one day flee away (Isaiah 51:11). Of that, the resurrection of the crucified Messiah is the sign and guarantee.

(30) Thursday

The Christ who has ascended

READ ACTS 1:1–11

When he had said this, as they were watching, he was
lifted up, and a cloud took him out of their sight
(v. 9).

After a period of time, which this passage sets as 40 days after the resurrection, the risen Christ finally left this earth and ascended to the Father. At the end of Luke's Gospel, this event was portrayed as following swiftly on from the resurrection (Luke 24:36–53); but it seems as though Luke was telescoping the narrative there, perhaps to make a theological point or perhaps knowing that he would return to a fuller account in his second book, the book of Acts. The theological point in question would be that the resurrection and ascension together are God's way of exalting Jesus and establishing him as one to be honoured and adored (v. 52). In Acts, Luke describes more fully how Christ appeared repeatedly and convincingly to his disciples over a reasonable period of time (40 days usually being taken as a round figure for such a period). In the church's calendar, Ascension Day is counted as 40 days after the day of Christ's rising and so invariably lands on a Thursday. This does not prevent the following Sunday from being celebrated as Ascension Sunday, and a good and joyous celebration it should be.

Most people today will have questions about the physical nature of the ascension as described here by Luke. Again we confront the fact that when dealing with the post-mortem experiences of Christ, we are in the realm of mystery, one that defies the usual kind of description. The picture of Jesus rising physically into the skies ought not to be deemed impossible when set against the even more extraordinary event of the resurrection; after all, none of these events could be described as 'normal'. The primary questions here are really to do with the meaning of the events and the place they have in Luke's testimony to Jesus and in Christian belief about him.

At the most basic level, the ascension marks a clear ending to the resurrection appearances. Until this time, Jesus had appeared in his risen form in a variety of ways and settings. These appearances were mainly to those who were closest to him, the apostles he appointed and members of his own family. From this point on, their testimony to the risen Christ was going to be all-important, relied upon by every other Christian believer. The appearances also established them as the normative and authorised interpreters of this new Jesus-centred movement. It was important, therefore, that there should be a limit to the number of those who were so authorised, in order not to create multiple centres of leadership. In this context, we can see how the apostle Paul might initially have been regarded with a degree of suspicion when he claimed to have seen the risen Christ: 'Last of all, as to someone untimely born, he appeared also to me' (1 Corinthians 15:8). Paul certainly had to assert his claim and therefore his authority: 'Am I not free? Am I not an apostle?

Have I not seen Jesus our Lord?' (9:1). But with the one exception of Paul, whose claim came to be accepted by the other apostles, the ascension of Christ marked the point at which the appearances came to an end, the reality of Christ's resurrection having been sufficiently established by 'many convincing proofs' (Acts 1:3). Now it was time to move on to the next stage of God's saving purpose.

In addition to seeing the ascension as the end of the resurrection appearances, we do well to see it as both the end and the outcome of the whole earthly life of Jesus. The miracle of the womb showed that Christ came to us not as the high point of human evolution but by the grace and as the gift of the living God. The miracle of the tomb demonstrated that the death of Jesus was not a defeat but a victory, and that the cross was God's strange but effective way of plumbing the depths of the human condition in order to overcome it and restore humanity to the divine communion. Death has now been vanquished and the divine image restored in humanity. Christ therefore returned to the Father who, in love, had willed and purposed the salvation of the world. Having come down from heaven, he returned to heaven. We are not, of course, to imagine that heaven is really 'up there', located physically above the earth in a triple-decker universe. It is natural, though, for earthbound human beings to think of God as 'above', 'in the heights' and 'beyond', because we wish to acknowledge God's transcendence, his otherness from ourselves and his divine majesty.

Christ ascended to the Father because everything that was necessary to do had been done. Christ could say on the cross, 'It is finished' (John 19:30), meaning that his bearing of our sins had been completed and that the whole mission of his life, to identify with and save the lost, had been fulfilled. The resurrection was the confirmation and proclamation of this fulfilment, and the ascension was the final sign that the whole earthly career of Jesus had reached its goal. Having come down to redeem, he then returned to the Father to indicate that the work had been done. The portrayal of Jesus ascending physically is, in fact, a picture of the theologically and spiritually satisfying nature of the work of Christ on our behalf. It is inconceivable that such an achievement should not be recognised, underlined and proclaimed in some way.

Some years ago, a number of thinkers took issue with the spatial language that the Bible uses to depict God. They argued that Christian thinking should take a turn in a new direction by eliminating what they thought were the remnants of an outmoded cosmology. The language of ascension therefore became an embarrassment. They were right to stress that God is also in the depths, since 'in him we live and move and have our being' (Acts 17:28), but this does not mean that language that takes us out of ourselves and makes us look upwards has no place. When we think of the exalted God, it is entirely appropriate.

(31) Friday

The exalted Christ

READ ACTS 5:17–32

> 'The God of our ancestors raised up Jesus, whom you
> had killed by hanging him on a tree. God exalted
> him at his right hand as Leader and Saviour, so that
> he might give repentance to Israel and forgiveness of
> sins' (vv. 30–31).

The right hand of a king or of God is the place of special honour and favour (1 Kings 2:19; Psalm 45:9). For Christ to be raised to God's right hand, therefore, is for him to participate in God's glory (Hebrews 1:3). The Apostles' Creed asserts that he is 'seated at the right hand of the Father'. In today's key verse, the apostle Peter boldly affirms that Christ was crucified, that he was raised and that he is now exalted at God's right hand. The God who spoke at the baptism of Jesus and proclaimed that Christ was his beloved Son has now demonstrated the fact that, after the whole course of Jesus' earthly life has been run, the Father still takes pleasure in his Son, so much so that he has given him the place of highest honour.

That Christ is so exalted leaves no room for any view of Jesus that minimises or reduces his glory. Among Christians, in the Church, Jesus is more than a fellow struggler who attracts our sympathy. He is more than an able teacher who had certain good things to say but other things of which we are dubious. He is not just a prophet or a sage who spoke with partial wisdom and correctness. He is more than one name among other names that deserve to be honoured. His is the name of highest honour and praise. He is exalted above all others because he alone is worthy of this position. 'For it was fitting that we should have such a high priest, holy, blameless, undefiled, separated from sinners, and exalted above the heavens' (Hebrews 7:26).

Of course Christians are entirely at liberty to find and recognise truth and goodness wherever they may find it. God is Lord of the whole earth and has never left himself without a witness (Acts 14:17). We are entitled to see signs of God's faithfulness to the world and signals of divine presence in many places and people. The revelation in Christ does not abolish the witnesses we find in other religious traditions and philosophies, so much as enable us to recognise them for what they are. Just as cats' eyes that mark a roadway are illuminated by the headlights of a car, so the light of Christ is reflected back to us in many ways and places. Yet Christ is central in enabling us to discern those ways. He is the criterion by which we know what is truly of God and what is not. He occupies the highest place in Christian estimation and is himself the embodiment of truth, goodness and righteousness.

The Christian message has a certain shape to it. At its most basic, it speaks of Christ coming down and then going up. Its implication is that he comes down to where we ar order to raise us from there to where we should be. T the shape of Christ's own cosmic career, of his journey into the far country of human sin and of his return to the Father's house. The honour he deserves is twofold. He is worthy of honour for who he is and has always been—the Son of the Father. He is worthy yet again for what he has done and who he has been in his earthly career. It is this that is recognised and affirmed when we say that Christ has taken his place at the Father's right hand.

The shape of Christ's cosmic career and the glory that is due to him are also recognised in the hymn of praise contained in Philippians 2. As we have noted more than once, Christ is the servant of God who humbled himself and became obedient even as far as death. Then, in Philippians 2:9–11, comes a logical follow-through: 'Therefore God also highly exalted him and gave him the name that is above every other name, so that at the name of Jesus every knee should bend, in heaven and on earth and under the earth, and every tongue should confess that Jesus Christ is Lord, to the glory of God the Father.' These words have given the inspiration for many hymns and songs and have shaped Christian liturgies ever since they were first penned. The fact that Jesus' name is the 'name above all names' is an established expression of Christian worship. It is echoed by many other New Testament verses, not least by Acts 4:12: 'There is salvation in no one else, for there is no other name under heaven given among mortals by which we must be saved.'

Perhaps, though, there is another way of reading Philippians 2. Is the name above every other name the name 'Jesus'? Or is the direction of the passage asserting that the name that has been given to Jesus is the name of 'Lord', and that this name is the one above all others? If this were the meaning of the passage, it would make sense, since the highest of all names is surely the name of God. God's name was revealed to Moses in Exodus 3:14–15: 'God said to Moses, "I AM WHO I AM"... "Thus you shall say to the Israelites, 'The Lord, the God of your ancestors, the God of Abraham, the God of Isaac, and the God of Jacob, has sent me to you': This is my name for ever, and this is my title for all generations."'

This name is also rightly given to Jesus. If Jesus Christ did not occupy this place of divine honour in and with the Father and the Spirit, it would be entirely wrong for Christians to worship him as they do. They might respect him, honour him or even revere him, but to worship him would be going too far: it would be an impious and blasphemous act. To worship him, as Christians do, is to celebrate the fact that he shares in and with the Father the glory due to God's name.

(32) Saturday

The Christ who mediates the Spirit

READ ACTS 2:1–36

'Being therefore exalted at the right hand of God, and having received from the Father the promise of the Holy Spirit, he has poured out this that you both see and hear' (v. 33).

The ascension and exaltation of Christ signal the end of one crucial stage of God's saving purpose and the beginning of the next. Because Christ has pioneered the way of salvation in his life, death and resurrection, the gate is open for others to follow him and enjoy its benefits. Yet this will not be done unless people hear and know of God's mighty acts and of the open door now available. The good news must spread. Today's reading records the events of the day of Pentecost, when the Holy Spirit came upon the Church in its inception and impelled it into the world of its day with great energy and spiritual vitality. Sociologically speaking, the modest origins of this major world faith were in a sectarian variation within first-century Judaism, which was itself a minority religion within the mighty Roman Empire. But its theological origins are in the eternal purpose of a good and gracious God who calls people to be reconciled to himself and to each other.

Jesus Christ is the mediator between God and humanity (1 Timothy 2:5). In this capacity he enables God to come to us and us to come to God. He imparts the knowledge of God to those who come to him and so is rightly called our high priest (Hebrews 7:26). The quality of relationship he forges between God and ourselves is one of 'covenant', of secure, abiding and faithful relationship: 'For this reason he is the mediator of a new covenant, so that those who are called may receive the promised eternal inheritance' (9:15). The blessings of God are all conveyed to this world through Christ, by whom he first made the world and then redeemed it. Here we are able to speak more decisively about the Holy Spirit. It was through the Holy Spirit that Christ came to us in the first place. It was by the Spirit that Christ was conceived (Luke 1:35), it was by the same Spirit that he was empowered (4:14, 18), and it is because of the Spirit that he was raised from the dead (Romans 1:4). We might truly say that Christ, in his coming to us, was the gift of the Spirit, the human being who came to us from God by the Spirit's power. But now the times have shifted, the gears have been changed and the ages have rolled on. The one who was the gift of the Spirit now becomes the giver of the Spirit. This is an essential aspect of Christ's work as mediator.

Christ's ascension to the Father is the point at which the threshold is crossed. Today's key verse tells us that because Christ has now taken the place of honour at the Father's right hand, he has received the promise of the Holy Spirit and has poured out this Spirit on the Church, the evidence of which was seen in the events of Pentecost. John the Baptist, as recorded in the Gospel of John, had spoken of Christ with the words, 'He on whom you see the Spirit descend and remain is the one who baptises with the Holy Spirit' (1:33). These words put it well and capture the priestly dimension of Christ's work. The Spirit descended and rested upon him and, because this is so, he is able to baptise with the Spirit, to impart the Spirit to others in his turn. If Christ's sacrifice is the means of our being reconciled to God and restored to a new life in God, then the Spirit is the transmission of the divine life, grace and power, with life-transforming capacity, into the experience of those who come to believe. If Christ is such a mediator, then we should go to the Father through him to ask for God's Spirit, in the assurance that those who ask for good things in his name will not be refused (Luke 11:13).

Human beings have always been hungry for spiritual experience but have often looked in the wrong place for it. Although many people have insisted that there is no spiritual reality, that all we have is the stuff of the material world and that everything else is illusion, human beings are largely reluctant to believe it. They have a longing for mystery, for transcendence, for that which cannot be measured and contained. Perhaps they sense that a world that could be reduced to cause and effect and nothing more would actually be devoid of everything that makes it interesting and profound. But not everything that offers itself to us as 'spiritual' is profitable. Spirituality should not be a product to consume, along with all the other commodities on offer in prosperous societies. True spirituality means being intimately related to God through Christ and therefore responsive to God's moral demand upon us, entering into holy and good lives that increasingly resemble the life lived out by Jesus Christ. It is a matter of being conformed to the image of God's Son, just as Christ was the image of the Father (Romans 8:29). This is possible only because Christ gives the Holy Spirit to those who seek him. The Spirit is God's agent in awakening us to our need of Christ, enabling us to participate in the life of the risen Christ so that we may receive everything he has done for us, and helping us grow progressively into Christ-likeness. When we enter the spiritual realm in Christ's name and by his Spirit, we do so in a way that is safe, that makes us whole and enables us to become not just good Christians but good people.

Christ has ascended and pours out the Holy Spirit. Being risen and ascended means that he is not limited by space, time or geography. He has left behind the physical and finite limitations that he shared with us in his earthly life. He is now without bounds, having become 'a life-giving spirit' (1 Corinthians 15:45), and so he can act in this high-priestly fashion for all people in all places. Through the Spirit he is 'the source of eternal salvation for all who obey him' (Hebrews 5:9).

(33) Fifth Sunday

The continuing acts of Christ

READ ACTS 9:1–22

He asked, 'Who are you, Lord?' The reply came,
'I am Jesus, whom you are persecuting' (v. 5).

At the beginning of the book of Acts, Luke described his first book, the Gospel, as being about 'all that Jesus did and taught from the beginning until the day when he was taken up to heaven' (1:1–2). Other versions translate these words as 'all that Jesus began to do and teach' (RSV, TNIV). The implication is that Luke's second book is about all that Jesus went on to do and teach. Today's reading tells of one highly significant work of the still-active Christ in the conversion of Saul, the Church's chief persecutor, who, in the identity of Paul, was to become one of the Church's chief advocates. We may see this event as a belated resurrection appearance. Paul leaves us in no doubt that he believed he had seen the Lord and had been transformed as a result. Furthermore, the ascension of Christ establishes the fact that this Christ is not controlled by the Church, as though he were some kind of commodity: Christ has ascended beyond the Church and, although active within it, is not controlled by it. He is free.

After the day of Pentecost, the risen Christ was active through the Holy Spirit in establishing the new Christian community in various parts of the Mediterranean world. Although Christian theology distinguishes the Spirit from the Son, there is no separation between the two. Christ is present and active through the Holy Spirit. Jesus had indicated that this would be the case. In John's Gospel, Jesus speaks about his 'departure' and then tells his close disciples, 'And I will ask the Father, and he will give you another Advocate, to be with you for ever' (14:16). He goes on to say, 'It is to your advantage that I go away, for if I do not go away, the Advocate will not come to you; but if I go, I will send him to you' (16:7). These words refer to the Holy Spirit, poured out at Pentecost to be the means of Christ's continuing presence in the world.

A number of details should be noticed here. The Spirit is described as 'another' Advocate. In Greek there are two words for 'other', one meaning 'another of a different kind' and the second meaning 'another of the same kind'. The word used here indicates that the Advocate is another of the same kind as Jesus. In other words, all that Jesus was, the Spirit also would be. This was not an alien spirit but the Spirit of Christ, the means by which the disciples would be held in communion with their Lord, even though he was physically absent from them. The Son and the Spirit are distinct but they are undivided and indivisible. This is why Jesus could say that it was to their advantage that he would go away: he would be replaced by the Spirit, who would make his presence known without boundary and without limit, wherever the disciples happened to be. This is the sense in which Paul can speak of Jesus becoming 'a life-giving spirit' (1 Corinthians 15:45). He did not mean that Jesus ceased to have a bodily existence (his risen body was still a body), but that by the Spirit he would have no limits to his capacity to be with the disciples for ever.

It is helpful to think of the coming of Christ in a fuller way than is common. In John 14:3, Jesus indicated, 'I will come again and will take you to myself, so that where I am, there you may be also.' These words are usually interpreted as speaking of Christ's second coming or, sometimes, of an encounter with him on the point of death, but we may distinguish three ways in which Christ might be said to come to us after his death. Firstly, he came in the resurrection: once his mortal human body had been transformed into a resurrection body, he came to his disciples to assure them that he had overcome death. He appeared to them and spent time with them in a series of mysterious but, for them, indisputable encounters that turned them from their disillusionment to a new confidence and courage. Then he ascended to heaven.

Secondly, he came to them again in the Spirit at Pentecost: he was with them in power, and continues to be with the Church in all places. Christ is therefore physically absent but spiritually available, and the assurance of his presence is repeatedly renewed in living preaching that speaks of him, in the celebration of Communion that is a regular place of encounter, in the fellowship of Christian people and the gatherings of the Church, where he promised to be especially present (Matthew 18:20). Christ is present by the Spirit without limit and acts freely (though not always, for us, predictably) in the continuing work of salvation in which he is engaged.

Thirdly, in the future there will be a final coming: 'For as the lightning flashes and lights up the sky from one side to the other, so will the Son of Man be in his day' (Luke 17:24). About this there will be more to say shortly. Essentially, however, the God of Jesus Christ comes to this world in myriad ways. It was said of the nation of Israel, 'For what other great nation has a god so near to it as the Lord our God is whenever we call to him?' (Deuteronomy 4:7). What was true for Israel is even more true for the Church of Jesus Christ in the age of the Spirit, through whom he continues to come to us.

The risen Christ continues to be at work. He works in and through the Church, which is his body. Although the Church should not be seen as the continuation of the incarnation (this would be to say too much), it is the body of Christ in the sense that it is where the risen Christ takes form among actual people. Having a body locates a person: this is where that person may be found and where he or she becomes accessible to the world. The Church is the physical community where Christ takes form in the world and becomes accessible. When Saul persecuted the Church, he was persecuting Christ. So, although in one sense Christ is absent, there is another sense in which he is very much present in his world, with his Church.

(34) Monday

The Christ who has authority

READ MATTHEW 28:1–20

Jesus came and said to them, 'All authority in heaven and on earth has been given to me. Go therefore and make disciples of all nations' (vv. 18–19a).

Here we find the words of the 'great commission', the command given to the disciples to proclaim the message of Christ to all the world. These words establish the Christian faith as a missionary movement. Some would translate them less as a command and more as an overflowing consequence: as we go into the world in Christ's name, we do so making disciples, baptising them and teaching the way of discipleship. Crucial for our reflection today, however, is the idea that Christ has been given all authority, that he is the supreme reference point for the whole of creation. The same idea can be traced in other New Testament writings: 'God put this power to work in Christ when he raised him from the dead and seated him at his right hand in the heavenly places, far above all rule and authority and power and dominion, and above every name that is named, not only in this age but also in the age to come' (Ephesians 1:20–21). Could it be expressed more strongly? According to Peter, Christ 'has gone into heaven and is at the right hand of God, with angels, authorities, and powers made subject to him' (1 Peter 3:22). What are we to make of this language?

On a personal level, we conclude that we should make it our first desire to allow Christ to reign over us. If Christ has authority, we should seek first the kingdom of God as revealed in Christ and let everything else find its place under his sway. Yet the exaltation of Christ does not change him into an authoritarian figure who bears no relation to the earthly Jesus. He has not suddenly shifted from the way of the servant into the realm of coercive power. Christ remains the same (Hebrews 13:8). What is vindicated and raised to the highest place in Christ is precisely the humble, self-giving, gracious way of being that we have found embodied in him. Raising him to the place of highest authority is the equivalent of saying that the virtues we see in him are those that will finally win the day. He is higher than all human powers, with their constant tendency to dominate and coerce as they seek their own interests and force themselves upon us. God's kingdom will come not by imitating the lust for power that is endemic to the human condition but by renouncing it. Although the nations roar and rage, they will not finally have the day. God is not in the wind that splits the rocks or in the earthquake and the fire, but in the 'sound of sheer silence' that seems so insignificant and proves to be so powerful (1 Kings 19:11–12).

When Matthew speaks of the authority given to a crucified and vindicated Messiah, he is, in effect, contrasting the way of Christ with the ways of the Roman Empire within which the Christian faith was born. The words here are meant to be subversive. Final power did not reside with the emperor, as was claimed, but with Jesus, and the contrast between the two could not have been greater. The emperor was the embodiment of human grandeur and of an imperial system that trampled people underfoot in pursuit of its own interests. Christ was born in a humble home and lived on the margins of the empire, seeking the well-being and good of others. Yet, so far, the faith that venerates Christ has outlived every empire there has been, and is set fair to outlast every other as well, along with their ideologies and philosophies. The early Christians came into conflict with the empire because they refused to say the words, 'Caesar is Lord' and declined to offer divine honours to him. They said that they would pray for the emperor but would never pray to him. For them, Caesar was not Lord; Christ alone held that honour. They believed that the Messiah outranked the emperor, occupying a higher place, and that, whatever the temporary setbacks along the way, the future would vindicate him and his cause. It was better therefore to hold fast to Christ and not to be dissuaded from following him. This was the ground of their great heroism in bearing witness.

Matthew's Gospel bears a now-familiar shape. In the first chapter, the genealogy indicates that as far as Israel, the people of God, were concerned, Jesus was very much an insider. He was a descendant of David and, before him, of Abraham. This was a fine pedigree. He belonged to the inside track of the Jewish people, who themselves had a special relationship to and calling from the God of creation. Yet this insider became an outsider, fleeing to Egypt as a refugee, barely escaping massacre at the hands of Herod, and then living in the obscurity of Nazareth as a carpenter-builder. Eventually he would die the ultimate death of an outsider upon the cross, enduring what was regarded as a curse: 'Christ redeemed us from the curse of the law by becoming a curse for us—for it is written,

"Cursed is everyone who hangs on a tree"' (Galatians 3:13). He even experienced what it was to be outside communion with God, as revealed in his devastating cry of dereliction (Matthew 27:46). So the insider became an outsider for our sakes, that he might identify with those on the outside and bring them in to the friendship of God. He bore the curse 'in order that in Christ Jesus the blessing of Abraham might come to the Gentiles, so that we might receive the promise of the Spirit through faith' (Galatians 3:14). In view of all this, Christ has been restored to the position of the ultimate insider, being given all authority. This insider then gathers all nations to himself through the people he has commissioned to represent him, the apostles and those who will become disciples through them.

To think of Christ in this way turns our world upside down. It invites us to reassess what is truly important to us. It leads to the reconsideration of every value we hold. Those who take the authority of Jesus seriously will be very different people, and the communities they form, if they truly accept Christ's authority, will be radical communities.

The Christ who reigns

READ REVELATION 11

---

*'The kingdom of the world has become the kingdom
of our Lord and of his Messiah, and he will reign for
ever and ever'* (v. 15).

In these words, John the Seer, author of the book of Revelation, has a vision of the future, foreseeing a day when the Lord God will reign over all the kingdoms of the world with his Messiah. The angel who speaks of these things addresses the Lord God Almighty and celebrates the fact that 'you have taken your great power and begun to reign' (v. 17). The paradox is that the Messiah who reigns has just been described as a Lamb that has been slaughtered, and has gained the right to rule because he has shed his blood (5:9). This Lamb shares God's throne and receives worship in the same words as are directed towards 'the one seated on the throne' (v. 13). The Lamb is also a Lion of the tribe of Judah (v. 5). The juxtaposition of these terms, the Lion and the Lamb, captures much that is both strange and wonderful about the Christian Messiah and the faith that he inspires.

Jesus Christ, to whom all authority has been given by the Father, is reigning 'until he has put all his enemies under his feet' (1 Corinthians 15:25). Yet you could be forgiven for believing that there is no benign providence that rules over the nations; rather, chaos reigns, or perhaps fate. Certainly international events are not under the control of human beings, who have let loose in the world a myriad destructive forces of their own making, which now roll on their way heedless of what damage they may do to actual people. It is not surprising that the New Testament speaks of principalities and powers that have become hostile to God (Ephesians 6:12). Whatever the 'elemental spirits of the universe' (Colossians 2:20) and the 'cosmic powers' may be, they are not human beings, and they have the power to override human endeavours and initiatives. People are caught in the machine of the market, or the world system, or armed conflict, or the powers that rule. From time to time, human societies are shaken in a way that reminds us how vulnerable we are and how fragile are the defences we build. The world desperately needs a ruler, and, hidden though his rule may often seem to be, its ruler is Christ.

To believe that Christ reigns in this apparently uncertain world is an act of trust, but it is reasonable trust, not blind faith. It is warranted faith. It is not a leap in the dark but a confidence in what we have come to know of God in and through the earthly career of Jesus. Christ's resurrection is the sign that not even the greatest power we know, the power of death, has the last word over God. The fact that Christ overcame death is the sign that 'neither death, nor life, nor angels, nor rulers, nor things present, nor things to come, nor powers, nor height, nor depth, nor anything else in all creation, will be able to separate us from the love of God in Christ Jesus our Lord' (Romans 8:38–39). Instead we are invited to believe that 'all things work together for good for those who love God, who are called according to his purpose' (v. 28). In the present age, Christ is reigning over the nations and guiding creation towards the day when his reign will have not only begun but been completed.

Some years ago, British commercial television carried an advertisement for *The Guardian* newspaper. Within a short 30 seconds, we were shown the same scene three times repeated—which I shall describe. In the first scene we notice a well-dressed man with a briefcase, walking purposefully across a square in the City of London. Suddenly a young man with shaved head and large boots rushes towards him and knocks him over. We draw a conclusion: surely the young man is a thug, mugging the man to run off with his briefcase.

The scene changes and we are standing at a different angle to the event. Now we can see that, behind the young man, a car is drawing up. Out of the front seats emerge two heavily built men in suits and, as the young man notices them, he sets off at a pace, knocking over the well-dressed city gentleman in his flight. We revise our judgment: this is not a mugging but an attempt by the young man to outrun the plain-clothes police officers who are chasing him. He collides with the gentleman by accident as he seeks to escape.

The scene shifts for a third time. Now we are looking down from above and we notice that, just above the city gentleman, a load is suspended and is in the process of slipping. If it falls, it will certainly be fatal for the gentleman. We now see what is really happening: the young man is rushing towards the gentleman to push him out of the way. He is risking his own life to save that of another. Then the words appear, '*The Guardian* gives you the right perspective on things.' We are left repenting of our prejudice against young men with shaven and large boots.

Because we are involved in the drama of life, we lack the perspective from which to interpret it in all its parts. When we are above it all, though, when time has run its course and universal history has been completed, then we will be able to look back upon history and see how its various components have fitted together. That perspective will come to us only when the words of today's key verse have been fulfilled. But we do have an inkling, even now, of how things will end, and that is given to us in the resurrection of Christ, an event of great finality. Through it we see that the apparent curse of the cross can be transformed by God into an occasion for new life. Here we perceive how God works, bringing something out of nothing, light out of darkness, joy out of tragedy, victory out of defeat. These are the hallmarks of Christ's reign and the warrant for our belief that Christ is reigning and will do so until that final joyous day arrives.

(36) Wednesday

The Christ who intercedes

READ HEBREWS 7:11–28

Consequently he is able for all time to save those who approach God through him, since he always lives to make intercession for them (v. 25).

The risen, ascended, reigning Christ to whom all authority has been given continues to pray for his people and his world and to make intercession for them. This is the ground of great confidence, as we also discover in Paul's letter to the Romans: 'It is Christ Jesus, who died, yes, who was raised, who is at the right hand of God, who indeed intercedes for us. Who will separate us from the love of Christ?' (Romans 8:34–35). This language is designed to instil in the imagination of believers a deep sense of assurance about the future. It indicates that, although the work of Christ on earth has been completed, the continuing work of Christ as he reigns is still in progress. The Christ who is now beyond our sight, but with whom we remain in intimate connection through the Spirit, is working towards the fulfilment of God's purpose. This is the meaning of his 'intercession'.

When the text says that Christ intercedes for us, it might be possible to derive the wrong idea. When we pray, our prayer is usually to do with things we deem uncertain. We might pray for guidance because we are confused, or for provision because we are in need. We might pray concerning troubling events in the world whose outcome is in the balance. The idea that Christ intercedes with the Father on our behalf might therefore be seen as problematic. Is the world's salvation less sure than we had hoped? Is the Father's attitude towards us unresolved? As it happens, these are unnecessary questions and anxieties. To understand, we should clarify what is intended by the writer of Hebrews. There is no question about the Father's attitude. When Christ intercedes with the Father, he is asking for something that the Father already wills to give. The outcome is already decided, but the means of delivery is still open-ended. Christ's intercession should be understood as part of a joint exercise of Father, Son and Spirit to bring to completion the purpose that has been willed from eternity and is even now in process.

In parallel verses, Paul says of the Spirit, 'Likewise the Spirit helps us in our weakness; for we do not know how to pray as we ought, but that very Spirit intercedes with sighs too deep for words. And God, who searches the heart, knows what is the mind of the Spirit, because the Spirit intercedes for the saints according to the will of God' (Romans 8:26– 27). Both Spirit and Son are interceding on our behalf and drawing the creation onwards towards its final goal, willing the consummation of all things. Christians may therefore be assured, to put it bluntly, that Christ has not ascended to the Father and then lost interest. The salvation of the world is still the project on which the triune God is steadfastly engaged; its completion may be delayed but has by no means been forgotten. Instead, we are in Christ's mind and heart as

Father, Son and Spirit together work to complete what they have begun.

To this we might add a further dimension. Christ is, in his very person, an act of intercession. We mean by this that at the right hand of God stands a human being who is the guarantee that he will be 'the firstborn within a large family' (Romans 8:29). He is the pioneer of our salvation, who is 'bringing many children to glory' (Hebrews 2:10). The fact that Christ has pioneered the way and stands before the Father as a whole, holy, resurrected and now glorified human child of God points to the fact that he is to be joined by countless others.

At this point, we need to divest ourselves of the notion that Christ's assumption of human nature in the incarnation was a temporary affair. To be sure, his life had a limited span on earth, but he has been transformed into an immortal existence so that he now is what we one day shall be. In returning to the Father, he has not left behind his human identity. Rather, he has taken it with him. When the Word became flesh, it was not for time alone but for the whole duration of eternity. He always lives to make intercession for us. This reinforces our idea of the humility of God, who has freely chosen to be eternally wedded to a human identity. It also reinforces the dignity of human beings, that quite undeservedly they should be exalted to participation in the divine life.

That Christ is interceding for us is more than an incidental detail along the way, an illuminating insight into how the ministry of Christ continues to be exercised. It is a theological statement. In the presence of God, there is a human being. He stands before God as the representative of all those for whom he died and for whom he pioneered the way. The human pilgrimage is not at an end. Neither does it end when our physical existence ends. Human life and potential cannot be exhausted in this life; there is more to us than that. It will take an eternity to realise what human beings are capable of. One day we shall be like him (1 John 3:2), and what he has undergone in being raised and glorified is what will happen to us: 'He will transform the body of our humiliation so that it may be conformed to the body of his glory, by the power that also enables him to make all things subject to himself' (Philippians 3:21).

The Christian faith sets at its very centre a particular human being and proclaims that God has come to us in him. In setting out this remarkable vision of God, it has also set out an astonishing appreciation of humanity. Its estimate of what it means to be human, of human potential and human destiny, will certainly be regarded by many as a gross overvaluation of this naked ape. The primacy that Christianity gives to humanity should never be taken as a pretext for undervaluing the rest of creation. But we should never think, speak or act with anything less than deep respect for each person, made in the image of God and with the potential to stand in God's very presence as honourable and honoured creatures of a loving God.

Christ will come again

READ 1 THESSALONIANS 4:13—5:11

For the Lord himself, with a cry of command, with the archangel's call and with the sound of God's trumpet, will descend from heaven, and the dead in Christ will rise first (4:16).

Earlier, we were encouraged to think about Christ's coming in three ways: he came to his disciples in the resurrection appearances, he came in the Spirit on the day of Pentecost, and he will come in the fullness of time to bring all things to their destined end. This final coming has been flagged up in episodes previously mentioned. At Jesus' ascension into heaven, the witnessing angels said, 'Men of Galilee, why do you stand looking up towards heaven? This Jesus, who has been taken up from you into heaven, will come in the same way as you saw him go into heaven' (Acts 1:11). So also Hebrews 9:28: 'Christ, having been offered once to bear the sins of many, will appear a second time, not to deal with sin, but to save those who are eagerly waiting for him.' Christians therefore expect a future coming of their Lord, which will be clear, unmistakable, personal, 'bodily', final, glorious, liberating and universally acknowledged.

Many of these features are in clear contrast to his first coming, which, though personal and bodily, was also ambiguous (people had divided opinions about him), hidden, humble, deniable, packed around with vulnerability and not final (although it was certainly definitive). The idea of a Messiah who comes twice, once in humility and once in glory, is characteristic of Christian faith. It puts clear blue water between the Christian and Jewish interpretations of the Hebrew Scriptures, while leaving ample room for dialogue between these two communities that are so significant for God's purpose.

The hope of Christ's second coming and final presence means that Christians live with a sense of provisionality and suspense. We are citizens of heaven (Philippians 3:20). We are caught between a great memory and a great hope. When we celebrate Communion, we look back to one who came in flesh and blood and offered his humanity as a sacrifice for others on the cross. We also anticipate a great feast that will take place in the future when he is restored fully to this world, a feast described as the 'marriage supper of the Lamb' (Revelation 19:7). We now live in the tension between that memory and that hope, and in this we sense the presence of Christ with us by the Spirit.

The tension was particularly heightened in the early Church by the emphasis on Christ's coming 'soon'. The early Christians prayed with urgency, 'Maranatha!' or 'Our Lord, come!' (1 Corinthians 16:22) and they heard the Lord reply, 'Surely I am coming soon' (Revelation 22:20). What, we wonder, would they have thought, had they known that 2000 years later the Church would still be waiting? But perhaps we mistake the point here. The 'soon-ness' of Christ's coming was more to do with theology than chronology. It expressed the urgency of what was at stake, the imperative to live for Christ and to make every moment count, as if it would be their last opportunity. It was a refusal to live complacently without reference to the demands of Christ's kingdom. The urgency of Christ's coming suggests that every day needs to be lived in the light of what is most important and that eschatology (the doctrine of the 'last things') is more to do with what is ultimate than with what comes last.

Christians have got themselves into hot water when they have failed to realise that the way the New Testament speaks of Christ's future coming is less in the form of a TV documentary and more like a series of impressionistic paintings. Christ's coming is glorious beyond our powers of description and so is conveyed to us in images that are vivid and symbolic. They are to be wondered at and appreciated rather than fitted together into a complex jigsaw puzzle. Christ will come, but woe betide those who take a literalistic view of how and when it will happen (Acts 1:6–7).

Today's passage is a case in point. Christ is portrayed as coming down from heaven, with believers being caught up in the air. Take this literally if you want to, but do not fail to notice the imperial imagery on which it draws. When a conquering Roman general returned with his captives and booty to Rome, the honoured citizens would go out to meet him as he entered the city along the Appian Way. Christ is portrayed here as a conquering hero, accompanied by a cry of command, the archangel's call and the sound of the trumpet. Yet the clouds mentioned are a symbol (as so often in the Bible) of the divine power and presence. The real ruler and commander, we are being told, is not the one ensconced in Rome, who, even as Paul wrote this letter, was probably plotting to persecute the Christians. Rather, Christ is the ruler of all, the true Lord who alone is worthy of divine honour, and the despised Christians are the honoured citizens who are privileged to share in his victory. How Christ will come is a matter that we may imagine in visions and images, but we should not speculate about it. The fact that Christ will come 'to be glorified by his saints and to be marvelled at on that day among all who have believed' (2 Thessalonians 1:10) is certain and sure.

A professor was once teaching about this passage at an African university. 'And what will he say?' asked one student. 'I'm not sure what you mean,' replied the professor. 'The cry of command,' replied the student. 'What will he say?' The professor thought for a moment: 'He will say, "Enough!" He will say, "Enough!"'

We read at the very end of the New Testament, 'See, the home of God is among mortals. He will dwell with them; they will be his peoples, and God himself will be with them; he will wipe every tear from their eyes. Death will be no more; mourning and crying and pain will be no more, for the first things have passed away' (Revelation 21:3–4). Christ's coming is our great and brightest hope.

(38) Friday

Christ will judge the living and the dead

READ ACTS 17:16–34

'[God] has fixed a day on which he will have the world judged in righteousness by a man whom he has appointed, and of this he has given assurance to all by raising him from the dead' (v. 31).

How should we think of these words? The role of Christ in the final judgment is spoken of in other New Testament verses. In 2 Timothy 4:1, we read that Christ is to judge the living and the dead, implying that this will happen when he appears in his kingdom. In Acts 10:42, Peter proclaims, 'He commanded us to preach to the people and to testify that he is the one ordained by God as judge of the living and the dead.' Christ is now God's gold standard, the one in whom God's expectations for human beings are made known and embodied in such a way that all God's future decisions and judgments for this world can be discerned in him and tested against him. Although the covenant laws of the Hebrew

Scriptures may illuminate us still, they are not the standard that now prevails, since they have been superseded by a new kind of law, one that is embodied in a person and ranks as the law of love fulfilling all subsidiary laws (Matthew 22:34–40). Christ is the true human being, the Alpha and the Omega of everything that God reckons as significant and good.

Yet judgment needs to be better understood. For many of us, the day of judgment is the day of final verdict, when the 'righteous judge' (2 Timothy 4:8) will deliver the knock-out blow, deciding who receives what, on the basis of what they have done and in whom they have believed (2 Corinthians 5:10). These elements must certainly belong to any biblical understanding of judgment, but they are not the whole and they are not the most important aspects. A judge may be better understood as one who presides over a process in which the truth is allowed to emerge. At the end of the process, situations are seen to be what they actually are, with positive and negative outcomes, or rewards and punishments, being apportioned righteously and with indisputable fairness. Biblically and supremely, the judge is not to be seen as one who is detached and impartial, the arbiter of some abstract principle of justice. Rather, the judge is one who works and acts to resolve issues and bring them to a just and righteous conclusion. God's judgment is that work by which God does justice to the world and its inhabitants. God's righteousness is not primarily the standard by which he condemns people for their failure but, rather, the action by which he makes people right, first with himself and then in their own lives (Romans 3:21–26). This judgment is something to be welcomed, not feared, since it means resolution of the world's confusion and distress.

All of Christ's work is to be understood within this light, since he is the means by which God has acted in the world to make everything right, giving him to us as an atoning sacrifice and as the one through whom we might be reconciled to God. Christ is God's means of restoring humanity to fellowship with himself. He is to be the judge of the living and the dead, in that the direction and content of our lives are now judged on the basis of whether we have entered into the relationship with God that he makes available; and, if so, to what degree we have allowed this relationship to be realised in our living.

Because Christ is the means by which God judges the world, the day of judgment is not a future event only, but a present reality. Those who trust in Christ and find themselves reconciled to God through him have the assurance that 'there is therefore now no condemnation for those who are in Christ Jesus' (Romans 8:1). For the Christian, the judgment is a past event: 'Very truly, I tell you, anyone who hears my word and believes him who sent me has eternal life, and does not come under judgment, but has passed from death to life' (John 5:24). To have been made right with God through faith in Christ means that what the final judgment is meant to bring about—namely, the resolution of the world's fallen and troubled state, such that evil is overcome and the grace and goodness of God reign supreme—has already come to pass in the lives of countless individual believers. All that remains is the completion of this process throughout creation, so that the whole world can be free.

God is merciful, and this is true even of God's judgment. God is merciful when he refuses to allow us to deceive ourselves about ourselves, when he rescues us from the illusion that we are the centre of the universe, without blame for the wrong that we do. God is merciful when he vindicates the world's victims, with whom Jesus identified himself on the cross. God is merciful when he confronts us with our failure to do what is right or maximise our God-given potential. God is merciful when he reveals to us that, in Jesus Christ, the one God has himself endured the consequences of our failures in our place. In the light of Christ, we can see ourselves truly—the person we have failed to be and the person we have made ourselves into. This is our judgment. In his light we see light (Psalm 36:9). It is better to face this judgment now and to embrace the path of recovery that God also offers us in Christ's name. The truth, unpalatable though it may be, sets us free (John 8:32).

Although the fearful images that describe God's judgment, both in the Bible and elsewhere, may sometimes cause us to fear it, the fact that we are to be judged by Christ should reassure us and indeed excite us. Who better to judge us than the world's Creator and its merciful Saviour? And who is better qualified than the Judge of all the earth to do what is just (Genesis 18:25)? Judgment day should be approached with joy.

(39) Saturday

Christ who completes all things

READ EPHESIANS 1:1–14

---

*With all wisdom and insight [God] has made known
to us the mystery of his will, according to his good
pleasure that he set forth in Christ, as a plan for the
fullness of time, to gather up all things in him, things
in heaven and things on earth (vv. 8–10).*

Today we complete Part 1 of this book and prepare to move
on to Part 2, in which we shall follow closely the events of
Holy Week, the last week of Jesus' life. Over 39 days we have
been on an extensive theological journey and have attempted
to explore the whole scope of the career of Christ, to embrace
in our thinking not a partial but the whole Christ. He is truly
the cosmic Christ, 'the Alpha and the Omega, the first and
the last, the beginning and the end' (Revelation 22:13).
These titles, applied to Christ in the book of Revelation, are
used equally of the Father and of the Son (1:8; 21:6), and
our readings over the past weeks have helped us understand
how this can be. In Jesus Christ we encounter the Word of
God, through whom all things have been created, who has

been made incarnate for us and for our salvation, who tasted death for us, was buried and was raised. He then ascended to heaven and poured out the Holy Spirit on the Church, continuing to be present with us in this way, reigning, interceding and working for the ongoing fulfilment of the divine purpose. He is the one through whom God is judging and will judge the world. We have moved from Alpha—the first, the beginning—almost to the Omega, the last, the end; but not quite. There is one final reflection before we change the nature of our journey and, in so doing, retrace our footsteps.

God has had a purpose from eternity. This purpose is for the whole creation and is being realised centrally, in and through Jesus Christ. Everything we have so far considered is part of this purpose. In few places is it more clearly stated than in the key verses for today. The mystery of God's will for the world has been 'set forth' in Christ, and it is all-embracing. The purpose is for the 'fullness of time', the end and goal of history, the undefined but still imaginable future. It concerns 'all things', a phrase that Paul frequently uses, which leaves nothing out: the mineral, vegetable, animal and human universe is embraced by it. God's purpose is to bring everything back together again; the implication is that fragmentation and alienation are the key problem in the universe. It is broken, in conflict with itself, and needs to be reunited and reintegrated. Yet this is being done in Christ and through Christ, who is the agent of reconciliation, renewal and restoration. The pathway to its achievement has been through the pain of the cross, but it is not only human beings that the work of the cross benefits: 'Through him God was pleased to reconcile to himself all things, whether on earth or in heaven, by making peace through the blood of his cross' (Colossians 1:20).

Christ is the key to the world's reintegration. His earthly life is definitive for us, 'final' in its significance but not yet final in time and fact. If Christ has realised the goal of God's good creation for us in his own life by loving God and neighbour with heart, soul, mind and strength, and if he is realising that goal in us by the Spirit through whom we have been awakened and by whom we are being made holy and whole, then he who reigns is now realising that goal with us as we move towards the Omega point of all things being united in him.

We might think of this creation as a project that God has in hand. It is coming from somewhere and it is moving to somewhere. On the way, it has to learn how to become what it is supposed to be. Christ is the teacher and the lesson. In him, the purpose of God has been 'set forth'. Human beings are made in the image of God and, as stewards of creation, they play a pivotal role. The progress towards the goal is not uniform. It proceeds as much by crisis as it does by process, yet the movement is purposeful, since undergirding it is the presence and power of the Spirit of God. The Spirit teaches the creation to resonate with Christ, to fall in with the rhythm he provides, to accommodate to the grain of the universe. God's judgment is a gracious and merciful work of confronting and refusing everything that creates discord and disaster. But the overall design is to fulfil the intended purpose, to bring creation home to the point where, being united with Christ and resonating with him, everything is 'gathered up' in him and finds itself for the first time. Christ is the one who makes all things add up: he is the centre and soul of every sphere.

The purpose of God is set out in the form of a logical sequence in 1 Corinthians 15:20–28. This passage begins with the resurrection and sees it as first initiating a new creation that engages human beings, creating from them a great harvest, then overcoming resistance to God's loving purpose on the part of the rulers, authorities and powers. Then comes the death of death itself and the subduing of all things under Christ. Finally Christ himself, the Son, is to be subject to God the Father so that 'God may be all in all' (v. 28). It is through Christ that all this is to happen. He is the agent of God's work, and the object is 'that the earth will be filled with the knowledge of the glory of the Lord, as the waters cover the sea' (Habakkuk 2:14). Rebellious human beings might shudder at the thought, assuming that such all-encompassing Lordship would rob them of their individuality and liberty. Those who have already tasted of 'the powers of the ages to come' (Hebrews 6:5) know that the exact opposite is true. To be mastered by Christ is to enter into freedom. To lose ourselves in God is to find ourselves ever after—and Christ is the key who unlocks it all.

Part Two

A journey of discipleship

(40) Palm Sunday

Receiving the humble king

READ MATTHEW 21:1–11

'Hosanna to the Son of David! Blessed is the one who comes in the name of the Lord! Hosanna in the highest heaven!' (v. 10).

Holy Week begins with Palm Sunday and commemorates the entry of Jesus into Jerusalem at the beginning of the final week of his life. Christians have celebrated this day since the end of the fourth century, when the custom began in Jerusalem of re-enacting Jesus' entry into the city at five o'clock in the afternoon. From Jerusalem, the custom spread to other parts of the Christianised world.

When driving in Israel today, it comes as something of a surprise to read signs outside towns that say in Hebrew, 'Blessed is the one who comes!' We are so used to associating these words with the entry of Jesus into Jerusalem at the beginning of Holy Week that we forget they may have been quite commonplace in his day. Yet they receive added depth when applied to this event, for Jesus is 'the one who comes' in very particular ways. He comes from Nazareth, where he grew up and where he learnt of his vocation (v. 11). He comes from God, being sent as God's messenger, the one who speaks for God. He comes 'in the name of the Lord' as one who brings with him the very presence of the living God. And he comes to fulfil and complete his ministry, which, as this week unfolds, we shall discover to be one of sacrifice and self-giving. Although, for much of the time, God may seem to us to be hidden, yet there are times when God becomes manifest and we can say, 'Here God is to be found.' This is one of those occasions.

It is possible to imagine that the events of Palm Sunday were spontaneous. Jesus knows, by some supernatural means, where an available donkey is to be found, instructs his disciples to go and find it and then sets out towards Jerusalem, to be immediately recognised by the crowds and acclaimed by them with the waving of palms. The alternative and more realistic account of this day is that it was a staged event. When visiting Jerusalem, Jesus was in the habit of staying overnight with his friends and followers, Mary, Martha and Lazarus, in Bethany, a few miles to the west of Jerusalem and beyond the Mount of Olives. He was probably staying there throughout the Passover festival, and some of the events of that week may have taken place in their home (Matthew 21:17). Jesus had already made plans for his dramatic entry by arranging for a donkey to be sited in a certain place at a certain time, and disciples of Jesus had been briefed beforehand on how they might respond to his coming. The palm branches they waved and strewed on the ground were symbolic of victory and of rejoicing, so the event is to be interpreted as a happy one, with disciples of Jesus welcoming his arrival and acknowledging his importance for them. They called him the 'Son of David' and, in so doing, were recognising his messianic status. They cried out, 'Hosanna!' which means, 'Save us, we beseech you!'

This word is unique in the New Testament but a related word with the same meaning is found in Psalm 118:25, where it is immediately followed by the words, 'Blessed is the one who comes in the name of the Lord. We bless you from the house of the Lord' (v. 26). This was clearly the text for the day.

As a staged event, the occasion can be described as an act of prophetic symbolism or as an acted parable. Jesus communicated his message in both word and deed. The entry into Jerusalem can be seen as acting out the messianic text found in the last book of the Christian edition of the Hebrew Scriptures, Malachi 3:1: 'See, I am sending my messenger to prepare the way before me, and the Lord whom you seek will suddenly come to his temple. The messenger of the covenant in whom you delight—indeed, he is coming, says the Lord of hosts.' Jesus acted out the 'Lord's coming' and, on arriving in Jerusalem, immediately entered the temple precincts (according to Matthew's version), where he engaged in a further dramatic prophetic act by overturning the tables of the money changers (Matthew 21:12–17).

For those who had eyes to see, the meaning was plain: Christ's coming was the moment of God's own coming. This was a moment to be grasped, with a response to be made. In his own way, Jesus was confronting the people and the religious authorities of Jerusalem with his own claims and with the way of repentance that he represented. Yet he was doing so without violence, since violence was the way he had rejected. He came to Jerusalem not on a war horse, to engage in battle, but in vulnerability and peace, 'humble, and mounted on a donkey' (v. 5). In doing this, he was knowingly putting himself in harm's way. He already knew what the outcome would be.

Palm Sunday recalls Christ's coming. The Christ who comes is to be received, and the tragedy of Jerusalem was that it did not receive him. Christ still comes. He comes each time the story of his coming is read or related in each generation. He comes by the Spirit to those who are prepared to receive him and welcome him as the Messiah, as the one who can save, as the Lord himself. The best way to begin Holy Week is by laying to one side the pride that says we have no need of him, by humbling ourselves before him and receiving Christ as the one who comes to us and for us. No human being on the face of the earth is beyond need of him. The way of discipleship begins when we acknowledge to ourselves, to him and to others that we too must say both 'Blessed is the one who comes!' and 'Save us, we beseech you!'

✟

(41) Monday

Joining with the
revolutionary Christ

READ MARK 11:11–25

---

*'Is it not written, "My house shall be called a house
of prayer for all the nations"? But you have made it a
den of robbers' (v. 17).*

Matthew, Mark and Luke all offer accounts of Jesus entering
into Jerusalem, and each of them does so somewhat differently. In Matthew and Luke, Jesus enters the city and
immediately sets about causing a commotion in the temple.
By contrast, today's reading from Mark tells us that, having
entered the city, Jesus went into the temple, looked around at
everything and, as it was already late, retired to Bethany. The
next day, he returned to Jerusalem and caused some trouble.

Mark's account of this event is also sandwiched within
another incident, in which Jesus curses a fig tree for its
lack of figs (even though it was not yet in season) and, the
next day, finds it to have withered. Some readers see this
as a strange and possibly uncharacteristic thing for Jesus

to do, since it appears both unreasonable and petulant. Yet it should be seen as another acted parable. The fig tree represents Israel, which is found to be barren of fruit and therefore attracts a curse upon itself. This is prophetic of the disaster that would happen to Jerusalem in AD70. Had the people responded differently to Jesus, circumstances may have turned out otherwise.

The fact is that Jesus was a revolutionary. This is illustrated by his physical action in driving out the animals and overturning tables in the temple. John even tells us that he made a 'whip of cords' (John 2:15). He was righteously angry, since the temple was being corrupted by the actions of the money changers. The temple authorities decreed that no Roman coins might be used to pay for sacrifices in the temple grounds because they bore images of Caesar. Instead, they were exchanged for currency that could be used. In the exchange process, however, the ordinary people were fleeced by the money changers, who, in turn, were in the service of the Sadducean priestly aristocracy. This was, in short, a massive religious scam (and there have been many others before and since). Money changing was only one of a number of money-making schemes involving those who had the monopoly in the temple grounds. A place of religious devotion had thus been transformed into an arena of self-seeking and self-interest, quite opposite to the generous purposes God had willed for it. This corruption was obnoxious to Jesus, as its contemporary equivalents should be obnoxious to us.

The incident inevitably raises questions for us about the non-violence of Jesus. It is often cited as evidence that Jesus was not a complete pacifist. It was certainly a violent moment, but it should be noted that there is no mention of any violence towards people. Rather, Jesus' anger was directed towards inanimate objects and to driving out cattle. Yet we cannot deny that this was a threatening action on Jesus' part and others would have felt him to be intimidating. We might find valid evidence here that Jesus was unpredictable, and that he was not afraid of risking both physical and religious conflict. Both of these qualities are, however, very different from the willingness to shed blood. We might also find confirmation that righteous indignation can be both holy and compatible with love. Real love cannot be apathetic in the face of gross wrongdoing. The people who were losing out to the money changers' system would already have been, for the most part, poor and deprived, and here they were being oppressed by those who should have been their shepherds. Jesus' actions were entirely congruent with his role as one who has come from God as a messenger and a prophet. In them we are invited to catch a glimpse of the God who should not be put to the test.

The importance of this event and the impression it made on the first believers is evident in the fact that all four Gospels speak of it. Yet John's account is quite different, both in the language used and in the position where he places it in his Gospel (John 2:13–25). Whereas, in the first three Gospels, it happened within Jesus' final week and contributed to the reasons for his execution, John places it near the beginning of Jesus' ministry, although still in the context of a Passover festival. It may quite validly be suggested that Jesus could have cleansed the temple on two occasions, once near the beginning of his ministry and once near the end (as the last straw!), but it may also be that John was making a point about the whole ministry of Jesus. In Jesus and his ministry, God has come to his temple (Malachi 3:1), only to be repeatedly rejected. In him, God came to renew and reform Israel, restoring the nation to its true vocation and mission. This was a spiritual, social and religious revolution. Yet God himself has been spurned in the rejection of Jesus and his message.

When people signed up to follow Jesus, they were throwing in their lot with a revolutionary leader and a radical movement. Jesus was so revolutionary that he overturned the concerns not only of the establishment of his day but also of their opponents who chose the way of violence. The way of Jesus was altogether different from the way of those who operated within the conceptual horizons of his contemporaries: it was a 'third way', a new thing that God was doing, and not many were willing to accept it. Although the Christian movement might easily be seen today as ancient, conservative and sometimes reactionary, authentic Christian discipleship continues to be about radical and revolutionary Christian living, which rejects all forms of religious corruption and ranges itself against wrongdoing and exploitation. These wrongs take different forms in each generation but are always to be found. As in Jesus' day, joining the Jesus movement means joining his revolution.

(42) Tuesday

Surrendering to
the service of Christ

READ MATTHEW 25:14–30

---

*'For to all those who have, more will be given, and
they will have an abundance; but from those who
have nothing, even what they have will be taken
away' (v. 29).*

The way Matthew tells the story, Jesus devoted a large portion
of Holy Week to teaching, much of the time in parables.
Matthew places the entry into Jerusalem at the beginning of
chapter 21 and then devotes five chapters to Christ's teaching,
which he locates in the temple (21:23), before coming to the
last supper in chapter 26. Among the parables Jesus tells in
these chapters is that of the 'talents'.

Once more, Jesus proves unpredictable. Having spoken of
him as a revolutionary, we now find him telling a story that
would delight a rampant capitalist. It is about the maximum
accumulation of wealth; at its climax we find enunciated
today's key verse, which, understood in the wrong way, would

certainly validate the inequities of the unbridled market. Some of the stories told by Jesus were quite risky and we can understand how he got himself into trouble through them. This story tells of a wealthy man who was going away and entrusted his property to his stewards. A 'talent' was not a unit of currency but of weight, and the sums mentioned here are consequently enormous, perhaps best captured in the idea that the master entrusted the stewards with 'a ton' of money— or two or five tons. He expected them to do something with the property they had been given. When he returned after a long time, he called them to account. Two of the stewards had done well and raised a profit. The third, being the last to give an account and probably by this time feeling very nervous, returned to his master only the amount he had been given. He had been afraid of losing it and so had done nothing. For this he found himself in trouble: what he had was taken from him and he was cast into 'outer darkness' (v. 30).

The ordinary Jewish people of Jesus' day might have had problems with this story. For them, lending money at interest was a very murky affair, associated with oppression and exploitation and very definitely with the Gentiles. The idea that Jesus might have been suggesting throwing in one's lot with the whole sordid business of making excess profits would not have gone down well. But a number of hints in the text indicate that this was not what Jesus had in mind. For instance, the wealthy man was about to go on a journey and would be leaving his servants alone (v. 14), just as Jesus was about to go away and leave his disciples. After a long time, he would return and call his servants to account (v. 19), just as Jesus will one day do, and the language of 'outer darkness' (v. 30) is redolent of the last judgment, when all people will receive from God what is their due (Matthew 8:11–12). These hints place the parable within the bigger story of Christ's coming and going away, of his return and the final judgment. In this way, it becomes a challenge not about the accumulation of material wealth but about the way we live our lives and use what is given to us.

For a start, we are only ever stewards of the gifts we have received, whether they are our natural talents (notice how the word has passed into the English language), our acquired possessions or our spiritual gifts. Whatever we have, we have been given, and there is no ground for boasting about ourselves or feeling superior. As Paul puts it, 'What do you have that you did not receive? And if you received it, why do you boast as if it were not a gift?' (1 Corinthians 4:7). Such gifts are not equally distributed: some people are gifted in many ways and others less so, but everybody has some measure of gift. What counts is what we do with the gifts we have, what return we are able to show on the 'talents' that have come our way.

On his departure, Christ has entrusted his disciples with gifts that they must steward. One of those gifts is the gospel itself, the good news of God's kingdom, which we are called to live out and to share. What we do with the gospel matters: do we bury it, keeping it to ourselves and believing only in its benefits for us, or do we share it and put it to work so that it is profitable in other people's lives as well as our own? When Christ returns, this is one of the issues for which we shall have to give an account. What have we done with all that we have been given? We are stewards and servants and, as such, we do not live primarily to please ourselves but to please the one who has the first claim on our lives and gave himself for us.

It should be noted that the third servant is roundly condemned in strong terms. He is told that he is wicked, lazy (v. 26) and worthless, fit only to be cast out and discarded

(v. 30). This language could seem disproportionate, but it was not the fact that he had committed gross sin that told against him, so much as what he had failed to do. He had been guilty of sloth, of being lazy, and in turn this stemmed from a fear of his master's reputation for harshness (vv. 24–25). Sloth—not being sufficiently bothered to be good stewards of what we have been given, hiding away our talents because our attitude is wrong—seems to be regarded by God as more grievous than we might think. The right attitude is not 'But I haven't done anything wrong' so much as 'What have I failed to do that I should have done?' Jesus' disciples are called to be profitable, to do something useful with what has been entrusted to them. Christ calls us not to miss the opportunity of living for him, of maximising our God-given potential in ways that will glorify him, and of fulfilling our calling to be stewards in the service of our Lord—who is not, like the man in the story, one to be feared but one to be loved. Surrendering to the service of Christ and being active in using what we have for the sake of his kingdom is an act of love.

(43) Wednesday

Standing under divine judgment

READ MATTHEW 25:31–46

---

*"'Truly I tell you, just as you did it to one of the least
of these who are members of my family, you did it to
me… Just as you did not do it to one of the least of
these, you did not do it to me"'* (vv. 40, 45).

Among the elements of teaching that Jesus gave during the
last week of his life are passages to do with the final judgment.
Perhaps, as Jesus neared the decisive, final crisis of his own
life, his thinking became more clearly focused upon the crises
that all of us face (the Greek word for 'judgment' is *krisis*).
Often, it is in the crises of life that we see which qualities will
stand the test and which will not (Luke 6:46–49). In biblical
thinking, there is a final crisis called 'the last judgment', in
which the truth is revealed, illusions are stripped away and
motives are laid bare. In today's passage from Matthew, Jesus
imagines a day when 'the Son of Man comes in his glory,
and all the angels with him, then he will sit on the throne

of his glory. All the nations will be gathered before him' (vv. 31–32).

Scholars have sometimes thought that when Jesus talked about the 'Son of Man' in this third-person way, he was thinking of somebody else. It is more likely, however, that he was thinking of himself in his glorified state, exalted and vindicated by God. Christ himself has become the criterion by which we are judged, and this is true in two ways. He is the criterion in the sense that his life is the measure of true humanity; he is also the criterion in that he identifies so closely with his own people—and, we might say, with the stranger, the naked, the sick and the imprisoned—that to care for them is to care for him. Equally, to neglect them is to neglect him. This means that no matter how loudly people might proclaim their own religious faith, the true test of whether their lives are really orientated towards God (which is what true faith is) is whether they display Christ-like living and compassion: 'Why do you call me "Lord, Lord", and do not do what I tell you?' (Luke 6:46). True faith makes us more truly human, and this means that we feel the sorrows and suffering of others and do something about them.

We make a grave mistake if we regard the Bible simply as a source of information. It is far more than that. The scriptures have been given to us not only to tell us something but to challenge us to do something, to shape our lives in particular ways. This is why it can be said that the word of God is 'living and active, sharper than any two-edged sword' (Hebrews 4:12). Teaching about judgment is therefore intended actually to bring us into judgment, to precipitate the sense that we are already standing among the nations under the scrutiny of the Son of Man as he sits on his glorious throne. We feel the weight of his assessment of us. Fortunately, as we do this, we still have room to repent, to amend, to change, to align ourselves with what is rightly expected of us. Although the passage precipitates us into crisis, it is not yet the final crisis. There is hope.

The correct way to read this passage, therefore, is not to see it as an excuse for condemning others into the category of 'goats' while defining ourselves as 'sheep', but to condemn ourselves in so far as we are guilty of 'goatish' behaviour. We recall that although we believe we are justified by grace through faith in Jesus Christ, the evidence of this belief is to be seen in the way we live, since 'faith by itself, if it has no works, is dead' (James 2:17), just as surely as works without faith are dead: 'For we hold that a person is justified by faith apart from works prescribed by the law' (Romans 3:28). There is no contradiction here, because faith is never rightly understood if it is seen as doctrinal assent or a mental activity alone. It is a personal commitment to Christ, as the Saviour given to us, that leads to the reorientation of our lives in a wholly new direction. It is not possible to have faith in this way without noticing it, without it transforming who we are.

About what, then, should we judge ourselves? The suggestion in this passage is that unselfconscious goodness is the product of calling Jesus 'Lord' and following him as a disciple. Jesus does not highlight the priority of right belief here, although other statements he made clearly indicate that we should be concerned about truth. Yet truth is never simply a matter of correct intellectual appraisal of a situation. Truth is a personal quality that is well captured in the word 'integrity'. Integrity is the harmony of what we believe with the person we are becoming. It is the consonance of our lives with what we understand of the God revealed in Jesus. Jesus himself, it appears, was not overly concerned about his own goodness. On one occasion he was addressed as 'Good Teacher' and responded by saying, 'Why do you call me good? No one is good but God alone' (Mark 10:17–18). This means neither that he was not good nor that he cannot be described as God incarnate, but simply that even though he was good, he was not conscious of his own goodness, only of God's. He was absorbed by God, not by himself, and this is a sign of true goodness.

In particular, this passage highlights for us the link between faith in God and truly humane, compassionate behaviour. Sadly, religion has often been used as an excuse for inhumane actions, the sacrifice of people for the sake of some religious principle. This can never be right and can never be a sign of 'true religion': 'Religion that is pure and undefiled before God, the Father, is this: to care for orphans and widows in their distress' (James 1:27). This statement recognises the ever-present possibility that religion can indeed be both impure and defiled, and stresses that the test of true religion is humanity and compassion. The words of Jesus bring us into judgment in the present and in our own consciences. We do well to examine ourselves in their light and align ourselves with Jesus' way.

✝

(44) Maundy Thursday

Sharing in the bread of life

READ MATTHEW 26:17–35

---

*While they were eating, Jesus took a loaf of bread,
and after blessing it he broke it, gave it to the
disciples, and said, 'Take, eat; this is my body.' Then
he took a cup, and after giving thanks he gave it to
them (vv. 26–27).*

On Maundy Thursday we recall the final meal that Jesus held with his disciples, during which he told them to remember him by holding similar meals in the future. The word 'Maundy' comes from the idea of a 'mandate', referring to the command Jesus gave to his disciples on that occasion to love one another (John 13:34). The meal itself grew out of the Passover celebration that was traditional at this time of year for Jewish people. The Passover was one of the three festivals in the year when Israelites would come up to Jerusalem in large numbers, and by it they recalled being set free from bondage in Egypt by the mighty act of God (Exodus 12:1–28).

Jesus took this existing meal and furnished it with a

new meaning. Now the focus was to be on a new kind of Passover, a celebration of the spiritual liberation that Jesus would accomplish through his own death and resurrection. He would now become the 'Lamb of God who takes away the sin of the world' (John 1:29). As Paul would later write, 'For our paschal lamb, Christ, has been sacrificed. Therefore, let us celebrate the festival, not with the old yeast, the yeast of malice and evil, but with the unleavened bread of sincerity and truth' (1 Corinthians 5:7–8). One of the things clearly suggested to us by this meal is that Jesus understood his imminent death in a particular way, as an act by which the forgiveness of sins would be made available to the world.

The Gospel writers all have slightly different ways of telling the story of the last supper. It is probable that, during the last week of Jesus' life, there were a number of meals that took place with the disciples and with different people present. John 12:1–8, for instance, tells of an occasion when Mary anointed Jesus with precious ointment at a dinner in her home in Bethany. On the occasion we remember today, Jesus appears to have made advance preparations to eat at a house in Jerusalem (Matthew 26:17–19). His closest twelve disciples are present with him. He divulges to them, to their great distress, that one of their number is about to betray him. We know that this was Judas (26:25). Despite this imminent act of betrayal, Jesus treats Judas as a friend, including him in the meal. John's Gospel portrays Jesus offering Judas a piece of bread, an act that counted as one of particular favour and friendship (John 13:26). So it appears that, even knowing what Judas was about to do, Jesus made a last appeal to him, relating to him as a friend rather than an enemy.

A great deal is conveyed by this action: the fact that God treats us kindly and graciously, even knowing what is in our hearts; the fact that while we are responsible for our actions,

God gives us the opportunity to behave differently; the fact that our acts of betrayal do not leave God nonplussed but that, in divine resourcefulness, God is able to make even our wrong actions work to the fulfilment of the divine purpose (Romans 8:28). In any case, it was not only Judas who was to betray Jesus. All of those present in the room would betray him in less active ways, by leaving him to his fate and by scattering like sheep whose shepherd had been struck (Matthew 26:31).

Whether it is in these active or these passive acts of betrayal, we should see ourselves. For all our fine words and protestations, each of us remains capable of betraying the one we profess to follow (v. 22). Like the first disciples, we are quite capable of imagining ourselves faithful and loyal, only to discover that we are anything but, such is the mystery of our own hearts. The mystery of Christ's death is that he gives himself for us and for many, and that the cross is the place where we can find forgiveness. Each time we share this meal, we return to the place where God's forgiveness is offered to us, and that place is the cross of Christ where Christ stood under divine judgment for us and offered his obedient and holy life as an atoning sacrifice to the Father. What we see here is the one God—Father, Son and Spirit—doing what is necessary to restore us to the divine fellowship. God gives us a place to which we can come to be reconciled to God's very self. Here God comes into our fallen condition and changes it from within.

Although there are many ways in which we can seek to explain this mysterious and gracious act, and each way will illuminate it more richly, we do not need to understand it to share in it. The fact of our salvation comes before our understanding of it. Perhaps this is why Jesus instituted a meal as one of the primary ways in which we can enter into the good of what he has done for us. At this Passover meal, he gave the Passover a new meaning. Taking the bread and wine (which would always have been part of the meal), he used them to express the fact that his own body and blood would be given up for us. Jesus did not need to be in Jerusalem on this occasion: he freely chose to be there, in order that he might give his life willingly as an act of ransom for many (v. 28). Eating and drinking the basic, simple and very earthy elements of bread and wine in the context of remembering him indicates that we need to internalise his act on our behalf, to acknowledge that it was done for us and for our salvation. A sacrificial meal is about sharing in the benefits of the sacrifice, having fellowship with Christ and others, in order that we might inherit the good of what has been done for us. Each time we do this, following the words and example of Jesus, the reality of Christ's saving death becomes real for us again.

(45) Good Friday

Trusting in the
undeserved sacrifice

READ LUKE 23:26–49

*Then he said, 'Jesus, remember me when you come
into your kingdom.' He replied, 'Truly I tell you, today
you will be with me in Paradise' (vv. 42–43).*

After the last supper, Jesus went with some of his disciples
across the Kidron Valley to the garden called Gethsemane
at the foot of the Mount of Olives. Here he endured deep
psychological distress as he anticipated the events of the
coming day. In the garden, he was arrested by those to whom
Judas had betrayed him and was successively tried before the
Jewish and the Roman authorities. He was mocked, scorned
and scourged by the Roman soldiers before being given over
to be executed. Crucifixion was a form of execution reserved
for political offenders, and this suggests that the Romans
saw Jesus as a political threat to their rule. He was crucified
on a site known appropriately as The Skull, along with two
criminals, just outside the walls of the city. The site is marked

today by the ancient church of the Holy Sepulchre, which, unlike some other pilgrim locations in Israel-Palestine, is widely regarded as being the authentic place where Jesus did actually meet his end.

The crucifixion is a sad event, but there is nothing about it that beggars belief. This is the kind of abuse of which the world is entirely capable. The cross exposes the depths of the human condition and implicates in the process religious establishments, political systems, the judiciary, law enforcement agencies, the irrationality of the mob and the cowardice of the 'faithful'. Not all these human agencies are always guilty of wrongdoing, but all of them have the hidden and demonic capacity to behave at their worst rather than their best, as history amply testifies. It is as though the forces of inhumanity gather at the cross, and, as he endures their assault, from the midst of the suffering they cause, Jesus prays (according to some manuscripts), 'Father, forgive them; for they do not know what they are doing' (v. 34). In this place of human rejection, Jesus lives out a different way as he refuses to be overcome by evil and instead overcomes evil with good (Romans 12:21). Here we see definitively portrayed the kind of behaviour we most readily recognise as 'Christian'.

All the Gospels record the events surrounding the death of Christ in spare, simple and sober terms. They do not dwell upon the details of what happened; they are remarkably dispassionate in the descriptions they give; the authors betray no signs of resentment or anger as they offer their accounts. It would be a strange kind of human being who did not feel moved by what they read here, but such people do exist. As there were those in Jesus' day who mocked and scorned him, so it will be today: human nature has not improved. But there will be others who are moved by what they read or hear, who will find something extraordinary in this record of unjust and undeserved suffering, who will find Jesus' willingness to endure such suffering freely on behalf of others both admirable and amazing, and will see beyond it a sign of the love of God: 'God's love was revealed among us in this way: God sent his only Son into the world so that we might live through him. In this is love, not that we loved God but that he loved us and sent his Son to be the atoning sacrifice for our sins' (1 John 4:9–10). In short, in this death we find something that saves us.

Jesus was not entirely alone when he was crucified: two criminals were with him. In so far as anybody could be said to deserve the appalling death of crucifixion, these criminals did—one by his own admission—although what exactly they had done is not known to us. In Luke's Gospel, one criminal dies deriding Jesus, while the other has a different response. There is something about Jesus that captures him. He recognises that he and his fellow criminal are dying because of what they have done, but that this is not so with Jesus. At the last moment of his life, he places his trust in Christ. He recognises his need of a Saviour and understands that Jesus is able to be that Saviour for him. He cries, 'Jesus, remember me when you come into your kingdom', and this is all it takes. Jesus replies, 'Truly I tell you, today you will be with me in Paradise' (vv. 41–42).

This is a profoundly Christian moment. The Christian faith is a movement of salvation. It is more than a moral philosophy of life, although it does contain profound wisdom for living. At its heart is the recognition of human helplessness in the face of ourselves: what we should be is not matched by what we succeed in being, and this dissonance is a chasm that we cannot cross. We only manage to fall short. The cross exposes the fact that we are locked into our fallen condition and lack the ability to lift ourselves out of it. We do not simply need improving, but we must be delivered from ourselves. Christ is the rescuer, the Saviour of those who trust him. He does for us what we are unable to do for ourselves, and at this point we are called to trust him. This is what many people find it almost impossible to acknowledge, but the dying thief recognised his need and cried out. He was certainly given the promise of a hope that went beyond death, since Paradise was a realm of blessedness beyond death. There was no way in which he deserved this positive destiny, but here lies the idea of an atoning sacrifice offered on our behalf by one who saves. It is for us and for our salvation that such a work has been accomplished, and we are invited to place our trust in this Saviour.

'Good Friday' is paradoxically named. Why should a day that depicts such human depravity and cruelty be designated 'good'? Only because the day confronts us with the truth and, however difficult it is to stomach, the truth in turn provides us with a starting point. By recognising what is true about ourselves, we seek for a way out, and Christ is that way, the one who has power to save us now and in eternity.

(46) Holy Saturday

Giving ourselves up to death

READ LUKE 23:44–56

---

*Then Jesus, crying with a loud voice, said, 'Father,
into your hands I commend my spirit.' Having said
this, he breathed his last (v. 46).*

Mystery of all mysteries: what was happening as the dead body of Jesus rested in the tomb and his spirit had been given over to death? The Jews reckoned the start of a day as being at sunset. Jesus died on the Friday afternoon and his body lay in the tomb (we may assume) until Sunday morning. Over the space of these days, Jesus was dead. The fact that Jesus did indeed die is clearly indicated. Our key verse for today tells us that he breathed his last. Even this was more a matter of Jesus actively laying down his life than having it taken from him: 'For this reason the Father loves me, because I lay down my life in order to take it up again. No one takes it from me, but I lay it down of my own accord' (John 10:17–18). Jesus freely gave up his life in sacrificial self-giving. He was dead and buried. We are well enough acquainted with what dying might look like, but what the experience of being dead actually involves is unknown to us.

We should not wish in any sense to lessen the fact that, when he tasted death, Jesus tasted it to the full extent. It is important to know that he has gone as far down as it is possible to go. The Apostles' Creed indicates that Jesus did this when he 'descended into hell'. Yet there is some confusion about the word 'hell', since older versions of the Bible have often used it to translate the Greek word 'Hades', which is not 'hell' understood as the place of final spiritual destruction. Hades is, rather, the realm of the dead, whereas the Hebrew word 'Gehenna' refers to the place of final destruction after the final judgment. To say that Jesus descended into Hades therefore means that he experienced to the full the experience of death. But is death the annihilation of life, a state of final unconsciousness, or is it some kind of journey into another realm beyond this one? That the latter is indeed the case is indicated by Jesus' words to the dying thief, 'Today you will be with me in Paradise' (Luke 23:43). Death is the end, but not the end. There is life beyond life.

Because we know so little about death in itself, there has been speculation about how we are to understand Holy Saturday, the day when the one through whom creation came into being was actually dead. One of the few biblical texts that we may draw upon to illuminate this matter is 1 Peter 3:18–19: 'For Christ also suffered for sins once for all, the righteous for the unrighteous, in order to bring you to God. He was put to death in the flesh, but made alive in the spirit, in which also he went and made a proclamation to the spirits in prison.' These verses suggest that after his earthly career, in the space between his death and his resurrection, Jesus had a career 'in the spirit', part of which involved preaching or proclaiming to 'spirits in prison'—which refers in some sense to at least some of the dead. This idea is reinforced in later verses: 'For this is the reason the gospel was proclaimed even to the dead, so that, though they had been judged in the flesh as everyone is judged, they might live in the spirit as God does' (4:6).

One interpretation has found in these words the idea that the work of Christ upon the cross has the power to save not only those of us who live after Christ's coming but also those who died before it. It might also apply to those who, in this life, never have the opportunity to hear of Christ, or even those who, having had the opportunity, never catch a true and proper glimpse of the gospel because of the imperfections of those who proclaim it. An understanding of this wider hope of salvation opened up by Christ must surely figure somewhere in our thinking, even if so much of it requires us to be agnostic. There are many things that we cannot know for certain, and this is one of them; but there are also many things we do know, and God's gracious and merciful will to save is among them.

Jesus died and, in doing so, passed out of our sight as he went on a journey, the journey of death. On this journey he was not abandoned but was accompanied by God's Spirit: 'For you will not abandon my soul to Hades, or let your Holy One experience corruption. You have made known to me the ways of life; you will make me full of gladness with your presence' (Acts 2:27–28). This is, I think, a passable description of Paradise. Jesus enters into the realm of the dead but is not abandoned there, because God's Spirit is with him. It is by this Spirit that he was 'made alive in the spirit'. In the same way, sooner or later, we too will take a journey into death, but we shall not do so alone. We shall know that there is one who has been there before us and has made the way safe. We shall be accompanied by the Spirit of God and of Christ and we shall not need to fear: 'Even though I walk through the darkest valley, I fear no evil; for you are with me; your rod and your staff—they comfort me' (Psalm 23:4). There is a shepherd of our souls even in death, and, as he leads us on the journey of life in death, we too can have a 'sure and certain hope of the resurrection to eternal life through our Lord Jesus Christ'.

On Holy Saturday it is a good idea to spend some time in quiet reflection and to imagine what kind of world this would be without the blessing of Christ and his coming. A world bereft of Christ would be a world empty of what gives it purpose, meaning, joy and hope. This is perhaps the one day in the year when we might choose to reflect upon that theme, and we should linger here before moving too swiftly to the morning that is to follow. The commonplace saying, 'You don't know what you have until you no longer have it' applies here more than anywhere else.

(47) *Easter Day*

Celebrating the gift of life

READ MATTHEW 27:57—28:15

'Do not be afraid; I know that you are looking for Jesus who was crucified. He is not here; for he has been raised, as he said' (28:5–6).

Here we encounter the solid early Christian testimony that Jesus Christ was raised from the dead and so was marked out by God as the name above every other name. Historians may debate the 'evidence for the resurrection', but no reasonable commentator doubts that resurrection faith informs every part of the New Testament and gave rise to the dynamic new movement that we call Christianity. The first Christians believed passionately in it and bore testimony to it even to the point of death. In fact, they were unafraid to die for their testimony precisely because they believed that the power of death had been overcome. Today's reading gives one account of the events of that mysterious day, an account that is supplemented by the other Gospels. The details vary but the testimony remains the same: Christ has risen indeed!

Can anybody prove that this is the case? Almost certainly

not. Can it be shown that the resurrection is a coherent and reasoned way of accounting for the available evidence? Yes, it can. Something happened that goes outside our usual frameworks of interpretation. At the very least, we can say that the early disciples experienced a range of visionary experiences and that they did so, on occasions, corporately. Visions are not unknown in the history of religious experience, although nobody seems to know how they work and what causes them. These experiences were more than visionary, however, since they involved elements of touch (John 20:27), they were prolonged over a reasonable length of time (Acts 1:3), and they involved different combinations of people in groups as well as private encounters (1 Corinthians 15:1–11). They were also congruent with external realities, such as the finding of an empty tomb that had been known to contain the body of Jesus, and the disappearance of his body. They were enough to persuade not only Jesus' disciples, but also members of his family who had apparently been sceptical about him, such as James, and even one person, in the case of Paul, who had been downright hostile (1 Corinthians 15: 7–8). As today's reading indicates, there have been alternative interpretations, such as the rumour that the disciples removed the body (28:13–15), or the idea that Jesus did not really die but revived in the tomb and persuaded the disciples that he had conquered death, or that something psychologically complex took place that remains inexplicable. None of these suggestions explains adequately what, in fact, took place. The resurrection remains the most compelling account.

Those who believe in the resurrection do so not on the basis of a high level of credulity or wishful thinking, but as an act of reasoned confidence that such a belief is warranted. The closed minds belong to those who will not even consider the possibility. At root, this discussion involves a parting of the ways between those on the one hand who believe that this world is all there is—that everything is potentially capable of a material explanation and that any occurrences beyond such an explanation are to be sternly dismissed as impossible and irrational—and those on the other hand who believe that there are mysterious realities in creation that transcend the merely material and physical while also comprehending them. When we speak of resurrection, we are not talking of an event that can be explained only in terms of this earthly reality. We are claiming that underlying material reality are deeper possibilities, and that resurrection is the manifestation of one of them. It represents the power of the future being made a reality in the present. The world is shot through with divine mystery and possibility, and is infinitely more interesting than the materialist allows.

Finally, however, those who celebrate the resurrection do not normally arrive at their convictions philosophically, even if they come to appreciate the strong arguments in its favour. They do so because they too have a sense of the presence of Christ with them, awakened either by the preaching they hear or by intense experiences of his coming, or in the still small voice that speaks to them in worship. The resurrection is more than a belief that good will triumph over evil, or that hope will emerge from despair, or that the significance of Jesus and his teaching did not die when he was crucified but lived on in those who are his followers, or that his memory lives on in the community called by his name. It implies all of these things, indeed, but is more than them all. Resurrection is the belief that this particular person, who came to us from God, for us and for our salvation, and identified with us in our lost condition, was not left in the grave or in death but was actually, not just symbolically, raised by God into God's own life, and was made manifest in space and time as the now risen Lord. All the language of angels and earthquakes and rolled-back stones expresses the wonder of this event and the fact that life would never be the same again after it had taken place.

Jesus Christ is the Alpha and Omega, the first and the last, the beginning and the end. The resurrection is God's confirmation and proclamation of this truth. Despite rumours to the contrary, Jesus of Nazareth, now risen and exalted, is more popular and more widely honoured than ever before, and with the best of reasons. This light shines in the darkness and, try as it might (and it is still trying), the darkness has never been able to overcome it (John 1:5). Christ is simply undefeatable and although his light is obscured from time to time, not least because of the inadequacies of those who profess to believe in him, it will never be put out. As long as this light shines, there is hope for humanity and hope for the world. The day of resurrection is, appropriately, a day of triumph.

Christ has died.
Christ is risen.
Christ will come in glory.
He is Alpha and Omega,
the beginning and the end;
the King of kings
and Lord of lords.

+

Questions for further reflection

Week One (Studies 1–7)

1. The studies use the idea of Christ as the 'key that unlocks the mysteries of the universe'. How helpful do you find this idea and how might it apply to your own life?
2. Consider the idea that Christ is both eternal and pre-existent. Why is this an important claim and what difference does it make?
3. If Christ is the one through whom creation has been made, how does this shape the Christian's attitude to the world of nature?
4. Belief that God is revealed in Christ makes a big difference to the way we 'see' God. Can you identify some of those differences?

Week Two (Studies 8–14)

1. It has been said that Christians believe in a 'downwardly mobile God'. How is this the case, and what difference might it make to the values we hold?
2. Christ is described as the 'bread of heaven'. What does this mean and how might this idea be related to the sacrament of Communion?
3. The studies say, concerning the virginal conception of

Christ, that although this was not necessary for Christ to be the Son of God, it is fitting and congruent that Christ should be born in this way. What does the birth of Christ from a virgin say to us about God and salvation?

4. Given that Jesus needed to 'learn obedience' as a human being, in what sense can we say that he was 'without sin'?

Week Three (Studies 15–21)

1. According to Jesus, the first and greatest commandment is to love God. For Christians, their prime calling is to become like Christ. How do we integrate these two central ideas?

2. Jesus is prophet, priest and king. Clarify what each of these aspects of his ministry means. How does each one shape and define our discipleship?

3. How might Christians take seriously what it means to have Jesus as our teacher? In what ways might non-Christians consider him a teacher?

4. In his day, Jesus overturned tables in the temple and caused a stir. What does he overturn today?

Week Four (Studies 22–28)

1. To what extent can we understand what it meant for Christ to suffer abandonment by God in his death? What does this say about our understanding of God?

2. A sacrifice is intended to cleanse from pollution. How are we 'polluted' and how does Christ's death cleanse us?

3. To see the cross as a place of reconciliation takes a leap of imagination. Can we do this unless we see that God's very self is involved in the work of the cross?
4. Historians can agree on certain facts—that Jesus died and was buried; that the tomb was empty on the third day; that the disciples believed they had seen him after his death. Is the resurrection the only way of interpreting these facts?

Week Five (Studies 29–35)

1. Why are the ascension and exaltation of Christ integral parts of the Christian story?
2. Why was it to our advantage that Christ left the earth?
3. Christ sent his disciples into the world to bear witness to him and to baptise. How are you part of this enterprise? How is your church fulfilling this commission both on its own and with others?
4. What are the signs in your locality that the risen Christ continues to be active in the world?

Week Six (Studies 36–42)

1. We should understand the ascension as Christ not so much distancing himself from the world as ascending into the control room of history. In the light of this, what does it mean for us to say that Christ is always interceding for us?
2. We are told that Christ is coming 'soon'. Given that 2000 years have passed, how does the sense of imminence affect the way we live?

3. Palm Sunday: On this day Christ came to Jerusalem as a humble king and, on the same day, acted with aggression in the temple. How do we reconcile these two very different actions?
4. According to Jesus, the temple had become a 'den of robbers'. A den is where people hide. In what ways might religious observance be a way of hiding from our moral responsibilities?

Week Seven (Studies 43–47)

1. Maundy Thursday: On this day Christ established the celebration by his followers of 'the Lord's Supper'. What does this Supper tell us about the meaning of Christ's death and why do we need to go on remembering this?
2. Good Friday: On this day the Lord of life experienced suffering, dying and death. Why do Christians regard such a tragedy as life-giving and full of hope?
3. Easter Sunday: On this day Christ appeared to his disciples and demonstrated that he had overcome death for ever. Outline the ways in which this event has shaped the Christian faith. How does it shape your life?

ENJOYED READING THIS LENT BOOK?

Did you know BRF publishes a new Lent and Advent book each year? All our Lent and Advent books are designed with a daily printed Bible reading, comment and reflection. Some can be used in groups and contain questions which can be used in a study or reading group.

Previous Lent books have included:

Giving It Up, Maggi Dawn
Fasting and Feasting, Gordon Giles
Journey to Jerusalem, David Winter
The Road to Emmaus, Helen Julian CSF

> If you would like to be kept in touch with information about our forthcoming Lent or Advent books, please complete the coupon below.

- -

❏ Please keep me in touch by post with forthcoming Lent or Advent books
❏ Please email me with details about forthcoming Lent or Advent books

Email address: _____

Name _____

Address_____

_____

_____

Postcode_____

Telephone_____

Signature _____

Please send this completed form to:

Freepost RRLH-JCYA-SZX
BRF, 15 The Chambers,
Vineyard, Abingdon,
OX14 3FE, United Kingdom

Tel. 01865 319700
Fax. 01865 319701
Email: enquiries@brf.org.uk

www.brf.org.uk

BRF is a Registered Charity

For more information, visit the **brf** website at **www.brf.org.uk**

Also by Nigel G. Wright

God on the Inside

The Holy Spirit in Holy Scripture

What does it mean to 'know' God? Far more than intellectual knowledge, to 'know' God is to engage in a personal relationship, to sense God's active presence in our lives on a daily basis—and that's where the work of the Holy Spirit comes in. The first Christians knew it was by the Spirit that they first believed and experienced God's love poured into their hearts. Since then, the third person of the Trinity has often been overlooked, even neglected.

In the last thirty years, however, there has been an explosion of interest in the Spirit. Christians around the world have realised how all experience is touched in some way by the Spirit's gracious activity. This book examines from the Bible why the Holy Spirit is far more important than most of us realise. It goes on to show that we need to take a fresh look at who the Spirit is and what the Spirit does—God on the inside of those who believe, on the inside of creation itself as Lord and Giver of life and, indeed, on the inside of God's own being.

ISBN 978 1 84101 484 5   £7.99
Available from your local Christian bookshop or, in case of difficulty, direct from BRF using the order form opposite. Alternatively, you may visit www.brfonline.org.uk.

ORDER FORM

REF	TITLE		PRICE	QTY	TOTAL
587 3	Into Your Hands		£5.99		

POSTAGE AND PACKING CHARGES					Postage and packing	
Order value	UK	Europe	Surface	Air Mail	Donation	
£7.00 & under	£1.25	£3.00	£3.50	£5.50	TOTAL	
£7.10–£30.00	£2.25	£5.50	£6.50	£10.00		
Over £30.00	FREE	prices on request				

Name _____ Account Number _____

Address _____

_____ Postcode _____

Telephone Number_____

Email _____

Payment by: ❑ Cheque ❑ Mastercard ❑ Visa ❑ Postal Order ❑ Maestro

Card no ❑❑❑❑ ❑❑❑❑ ❑❑❑❑ ❑❑❑❑ ❑❑❑

Valid from ❑❑❑❑ Expires ❑❑❑❑ Issue no. ❑❑❑

Security code* ❑❑❑ *Last 3 digits on the reverse of the card. ESSENTIAL IN ORDER TO PROCESS YOUR ORDER Shaded boxes for Maestro use only

Signature _____ Date _____

All orders must be accompanied by the appropriate payment.

Please send your completed order form to:
BRF, 15 The Chambers, Vineyard, Abingdon OX14 3FE
Tel. 01865 319700 / Fax. 01865 319701 Email: enquiries@brf.org.uk

❑ Please send me further information about BRF publications.

Available from your local Christian bookshop.   BRF is a Registered Charity

About
brf:

BRF is a registered charity and also a limited company, and has been in existence since 1922. Through all that we do—producing resources, providing training, working face-to-face with adults and children, and via the web—we work to resource individuals and church communities in their Christian discipleship through the Bible, prayer and worship.

Our Barnabas children's team works with primary schools and churches to help children under 11, and the adults who work with them, to explore Christianity creatively and to bring the Bible alive.

To find out more about BRF and its core activities and ministries, visit:

www.brf.org.uk
www.brfonline.org.uk
www.barnabasinschools.org.uk
www.barnabasinchurches.org.uk
www.messychurch.org.uk
www.foundations21.org.uk

If you have any questions about BRF and our work, please email us at

enquiries@brf.org.uk